PAUL THE

George Appleton has had a long, varied and adventurous ministry, beginning as a curate in Stepney in 1925, followed by nearly 20 years as a missionary in Burma, then as a priest in Harrow, after which he served for eight years as an ecumenical missionary secretary, gaining a knowledge of the worldwide Church and of other communities of faith. Five years as a City rector were followed by a short period as Archdeacon of London and Canon of St Paul's Cathedral. From there he was called to Western Australia to become Archbishop of Perth; six years later he became Anglican Archbishop in Jerusalem. Now in retirement he reflects on the discipleship which has been at the heart of this varied experience.

GEORGE APPLETON

Paul
The Interpreter

George Appleton

Collins
FOUNT PAPERBACKS

First published in Great Britain by
Fount Paperbacks, London in 1989

Copyright © George Appleton 1989

Printed and bound in Great Britain by
William Collins Sons & Co. Ltd, Glasgow

Contents

For Priscilla, Lady Collins
in grateful recognition of
her inspiration and devoted development
of Fount Paperbacks.

Acknowledgements

Unless otherwise specified, bible quotations are taken from the Revised Standard Version Bible, copyright 1946, 1952, 1971 by the Division of Christian Education of the National Council of the Churches of Christ in the USA, and is used by permission.

Abbreviations

AV   The Authorized (King James) Version of the Bible
GNB   The Good News Bible
JB   The Jerusalem Bible
NEB   The New English Bible
RSV   The Revised Standard Version of the Bible

Introduction

"We learn what Christ is from the man who, though he knew not Christ after the flesh, divined better than any what Christ stood and stands for."

So wrote C. H. Dodd, the great scholar of the New Testament, when as a young man in 1929 he determined to recover Paul's essential thought out of its obsolete form which, though understandable in Paul's own day, needs to be expressed in the living language of today. That is how most of us, nearly two thousand years after Paul, need to interpret Jesus the Christ, whom the writer of the epistle to the Hebrews spoke of as, "Jesus Christ, the same yesterday and today and for ever" (13:8). Paul is the greatest interpreter of Christ, the one who first realized his cosmic or univeral significance.

Why then is another book necessary if C. H. Dodd's little masterpiece, *The Meaning of Paul for Today*, is so satisfying, reinforced as it is in Charles Raven's paperback *St Paul and the Gospel of Jesus* (1961)?

The Risen Jesus is the same. Paul in the spiritual and eternal pleroma or fullness into which he entered when he was beheaded around the mid-sixties AD now knows and understands fully, even as he was fully understood and known by God (1 Corinthians

13:12). We in the closing years of the twentieth century know much more about the world, creation and the people living in it, than any earlier generation. Biblical scholars have helped us to understand the great texts of the scriptures, and the scriptures themselves have been translated into over a thousand languages. Radio tells us what is happening in the world a few minutes after events have happened. Television enables us to look through a window, as it were, and see how people live and behave, their sacred places and the buildings they set apart for prayer and worship. With aeroplanes flying with the speed of sound and the rapid advances in technology, to say nothing of nuclear weapons and the remote detonation of hidden bombs, we seem to be living in a different world to that of Jesus, Paul, Dodd and Raven.

This small and very personal book attempts to see how it all relates to our knowledge of ourselves, our faith and trust in God, the religious traditions that have been handed down to us, and our ideas of the good life that is necessary if the nations are to live together in peace and justice and human rights are to be enjoyed by all.

Knowing the way I tend to skip over Bible references where just chapter and verse are enumerated, I have given the full quotation in each case. This has helped me to delve more deeply into what Paul is trying to say, and also to link up his sequence of thought.

I have also not hesitated to repeat points Paul

makes in different contexts. Quite often he wants Christians in different places to reflect on the issues he is setting forth, for in the main he is answering questions put to him in one letter, in a way that will be relevant to others. Occasionally I have put a second thought before an earlier one, as the writer of a letter will do when the mention of a point reminds him of something which might have come better earlier. Neither Paul nor his amanuensis had the advantage of a word processor which could correct mistakes or alter the order of paragraphs to make the point in question flow more easily. Often his writing is like the composition of a piece of music where a key phrase is repeated, as in a fugue.

I have come to see Paul as the great interpreter of Christ and the first writer to see his universal message. He felt a call to be responsible for the Gentile world, far and away the greater section of mankind. He saw that salvation was God's free gift. No one could earn or deserve it; no code of conduct, however meticulously observed, could win it. People to whom I have mentioned this study have frankly admitted that they do not understand Paul, nor do their hearts warm to him when they hear passages from his epistles read in church services. I myself have admired him, but I have not until recently regarded him as both loving and loveable, in spite of the one passage of his that is read most often, namely the thirteen verses on love in chapter thirteen of his first letter to the group of converts in Corinth. My hope is that readers of this short book will relate it to their own lives, see the deep contribution that Paul has made to the religious life of mankind, and see his relevance to our life, thought and spiritual experience today.

1

Paul on Himself

If only Paul had written an autobiography our task of understanding his life story would have been comparatively easy. If one of his intimate companions had written an authorized biography, after several hours of careful reading we might have reached similar conclusions. Instead we have to study the letters he wrote, probably over a period of fifteen years, and the accounts of his journeys which his Gentile friend and medical adviser Luke included in the first church history which we know as the Acts of the Apostles.

In almost all the versions of the Bible, ancient and modern, and in the modern translations into over a thousand languages, the order of the epistles is based on their respective lengths, beginning with Romans and ending with Philemon, rather than the order in which they were written. This makes it difficult for most readers to see the development of Paul's thought or appreciate his expanding pastoral responsibility as the churches founded by him grew in numbers and new Christians sought to establish a relationship with the society in which they lived.

Another feature that we need to keep in mind is

that with the exception of Romans and Ephesians, Paul's epistles are not theological treatises, but letters. They deal with questions raised by the new believers concerning Jesus as the long-awaited Messiah, or with matters about which Paul wished to give encouragement, warning or even rebuke. So in this opening chapter we shall study the epistles in the order in which they were written, paying particular attention to what Paul says in his opening greetings and in his closing mentions of personal friends and fellow-workers.

One thing that Paul is always eager to claim is that his faith in Christ came not through human agents but in direct revelation from God and in experience of the Risen Christ. He is an apostle in the same way as the first twelve Apostles. The Church down the centuries has always accepted that Paul and Barnabas were sent out into the world by the Christians of Antioch acting under the inspiration of the Holy Spirit. Luke records, "while they were worshipping the Lord and fasting, the Holy Spirit said, 'Set apart for me Barnabas and Saul for the work to which I have called them.' Then after fasting and praying they laid their hands on them and sent them off" (Acts 13:2–3).

New Testament scholars think that Saul was born in the first decade of the AD reckoning, so that he and Jesus were contemporaries though there is no clear evidence that they ever met in the flesh. There is general agreement that Paul was converted to Christ in the year AD 34, was first imprisoned in

Rome in AD 61–63, and was martyred during Nero's persecution in AD 67. So Paul was around sixty years of age when he died. The order in which the epistles were written could well have been:

AD 50–51	1 and 2 Thessalonians
AD 57	1 and 2 Corinthians
AD 57–58	Galatians and Romans
AD 61–63	Ephesians, Philippians, Colossians and Philemon

The two epistles to Timothy and that to Titus are thought by some scholars to have been written in the period AD 65–80. This raises the question of whether they were written by Paul himself or in his name by someone close to him, or by someone wishing to have his authority.

Another consideration that we need to keep in mind is that of what are called the "we" passages in Acts. These appear to be a kind of travel diary of the writer of Acts, generally assumed to be Luke. In the opening verses he speaks of the care which he exercised in its compilation:

> In the first book, O Theophilus, I have dealt with all that Jesus began to do and teach, until the day when he was taken up, after he had given commandment through the Holy Spirit to the apostles whom he had chosen. To them he presented himself alive after his passion by many proofs, appearing to them during forty days, and speaking of the kingdom of God.

> And while staying with them he charged them
> not to depart from Jerusalem, but to wait for
> the promise of the Father, which, he said,
> "you heard from me". (Acts 1:1–4)

The opening paragraphs of both Luke and Acts are
addressed to "most excellent Theophilus", which
could indicate a Roman official of governor rank,
whom the writer knew personally, possibly also
known to Paul. Alternatively the name "Theophilus", meaning literally "a lover of God", might
represent Roman officials, God-fearers who felt more
attracted to Jewish belief in a transcendent and righteous God than to the idolatrous and immoral gods of
Roman mythology. The writer of the gospel wanted
to record what he had picked up from eye-witnesses
of Jesus and accredited ministers. In his second book
he aimed at showing that the same kind of things
were happening as he had spoken of in the first book.
This second book took his readers up to Paul's arrival
at Rome, the capital of the empire. It is quite
possible, even probable, that he intended to write a
third volume, dealing with Paul's doings after his
release from a first imprisonment and culminating in
his martyrdom in AD 67. What prevented him from
writing this third volume we can only conjecture.

I have spoken somewhat tentatively of Luke's
authorship of the third gospel, for his name is not
mentioned in the earliest manuscripts. This is not the
place to describe in detail how he came to be identi-
fied as the author. He may be the brother not named

in 2 Corinthians 8:18, "who is famous among all the churches for his preaching of the gospel". In two other contexts Luke is specifically mentioned: "Only Luke is with me" (2 Timothy 4:11), perhaps written by Paul himself; and, "Luke the beloved physician and Demas greet you" (Colossians 4:14). The third gospel had not been written at the time of these mentions, but anyone who aimed at writing a gospel must have had it much in mind before he got down to the actual task of writing.

Paul himself in the letter to the Galatians gives some biographical background and reflections: "I advanced in Judaism beyond many of my own age among my people so extremely zealous was I for the traditions of my fathers". He goes on to speak of his vocation to take the gospel to the Gentiles, a vocation first perceived by the somewhat fearful disciple Ananias, who felt that Christ was prompting him to go and visit this notorious persecutor who was said to have arrived at Damascus after a mysterious experience on the outskirts of the city which had left him collapsed and blind. It is interesting that the same idea seems to have come to both Ananias and Saul at the same time, a conviction that only began to be fulfilled years later. Hindsight probably clarified memories in both Paul and Luke, and helped both to recognize the seed from which both growth and development took place (Galatians 1:11–17; Acts 9:10–18). Also in the original experience of both was the hint that such a tremendous vocation would only be fulfilled with much suffering.

It seems to have taken years before the meaning of the Damascus happening became clear to Paul. He tells us that a few days after it he went away into Arabia, the countryside around Damascus, where he stayed for three years before going up to Jerusalem (Galatians 1:17–18). Fourteen years elapsed before he went up again to Jerusalem with Barnabas and Titus to lay before the leaders of the church the message he had been preaching to the Gentiles (Galatians 2:1). A considerable part of this time had been spent in Tarsus working out the implications of his Damascus experience, until Barnabas arrived to invite him to Antioch, where the disciples were thinking of a mission to the outside world (Acts 11:25–26).

Paul was always emphatic in his claim that his call to be a disciple came direct from Christ and not from any human source. Yet he was humble about it: "For I am the least of the apostles, unfit to be called an apostle, because I persecuted the church of God. But by the grace of God I am what I am, and his grace toward me was not in vain" (1 Corinthians 15:9–10).

In more than one of his epistles he speaks of himself as a servant of Christ Jesus (e.g. Romans 1:1), and sometimes his use of the word "servant" would suggest "slave". In Luke's account of the shipwreck on the voyage to Rome, Paul encourages the crew: "For this very night there stood by me an angel of the God to whom I belong and whom I worship" (Acts 27:23). The early intuitions of probable suffering are seen and accepted. "I rejoice in my sufferings which make up what is lacking in Christ's sufferings" (Colossians 1:24). Few of Christ's disciples in any generation or time of hostility would dare to say the second part of this devotional discipleship, though more of us might be able to say truly that we rejoice in sharing in these sufferings, being strengthened by grace to endure them.

The following chapters in this small book will try to work out in more detail and deeper implication some of the facts of the life of this amazing disciple.

2

The Turning Point

Paul always insisted that his conversion was brought about by a personal experience of the Risen Christ, and that his call to be an apostle to the Gentiles, the vast majority of the world's inhabitants, came directly from God. In the opening verse of his first letter to the Christians of Corinth he speaks of being "called by the will of God to be an apostle of Christ Jesus". The beginning of his second letter says the same. To the yet unvisited Christians of Rome, he calls himself "a servant of Jesus Christ, called to be an apostle, set apart for the gospel of God", who had been promised beforehand through God's prophets in the holy scriptures. The opening sentence of the letter to the churches of Galatia is even more explicit: "Paul an apostle – not from men nor through man, but through Jesus Christ and God the Father".

The one person who could be thought of as God's human agent is Stephen whom Paul, looking back after his rescue from the riotous Jews in Jerusalem, spoke of as "the Lord's martyr" (AV) or "the Lord's witness" (RSV, NEB, JB). For the whole of Paul's speech, see Luke's account in Acts 22:1–21.

Stephen is first mentioned when the Jewish Christians born outside Palestine complained that their widows and poor were not getting their fair share in the daily distribution of charitable relief. The twelve apostles gathered the whole body together and explained that they regarded their main task to be preaching the good news and praying. They therefore suggested that seven men, well-spoken of, wise and spiritually minded, should be chosen to carry out this "service of tables", leaving themselves free to carry on their spiritual priorities. This pleased the whole group who then chose seven men (not actually called "deacons") and brought them to the Twelve, who prayed over them and laid their hands upon them.

The first named of the seven was Stephen, "full of grace and power", who, in addition to taking part in the charitable ministrations, was an inspired preacher of the gospel and a worker of miracles. His effective ministry aroused opposition from the synagogues in Jerusalem, whose members arrested him and brought him before the Sanhedrin. "False witnesses" accused him of blasphemous words against Moses and the Temple, saying that they had heard him say that Jesus would change the customs. Studying Luke's description of the trial (Acts 6 and 7) one would think that these "false witnesses" had perceived something that was true rather than false, namely that discipleship under Jesus involved a change of heart and life style both for the individual disciple and the corporate body.

Called upon by the high priest, Stephen gave a summary of the history of God's operation from the time of Abraham down to the contemporary situation, concentrating particularly on Abraham, Joseph and Moses, and bringing out the point that Abraham was uncircumcized when he experienced God's revelation. Stephen went on to speak of the temple that Solomon built, making it clear that "the Most High does not dwell in houses made with hands". He then quoted from Isaiah 66:1–2: "Thus says the Lord: 'Heaven is my throne and the earth is my footstool; what is the house which you would build for me, and what is the place of my rest? All these things my hand has made, and so all these things are mine'." The word "rest" seems to mean "permanent residence", almost a localised presence.

Stephen also claimed that Israel had not offered regular sacrifices in their forty years in the wilderness, but had worshipped Moloch and Rephan (Acts 7:43). He also reminded his judges of the promise that Moses had made, that God would raise up a prophet from among themselves like him, implying that Jesus was the promised successor (Acts 7:37). Summing up, he claimed that Israel had always been a stiff-necked people, uncircumcised in heart or ears, for ever resisting the Holy Spirit, persecuting the prophets who proclaimed the coming of the Righeous One whom they had betrayed and murdered, and never keeping the Law.

As Stephen finished his defence, the author of Acts tells us that he looked up to heaven with rapture in his eyes, saw the glory of God, and Jesus at the right hand of God, the place of authority and power, standing to strengthen and receive his faithful witness. Luke, whose aim was to gather carefully the facts of the life of Jesus and the early days of the Church, says that there was a look on Stephen's face which spoke of a message from God and a smile of joy in being that chosen messenger. With his final denunciation and conviction of vision it is no wonder that Stephen's hearers were enraged and threw him out of the city and stoned him to death.

Stephen's joyful conviction of vision in the court of his trial continued through the rushed short journey outside the city and through the violence of his stoning: "I see the heavens opened and Jesus standing at the right hand of God". At this, the enraged persecutors stopped their ears and hurled their lumps of rock more violently. Stephen knelt down and prayed, "Lord Jesus, receive my spirit". His last words showed his determination to die in the same way that his master had done in the long drawn out agony on the cross: "Lord, do not hold this sin against them". The first martyr was a witness full of faith, whose devoted imitation of his Lord continued to the last seconds of life.

Saul must have heard the detailed speech recorded by Luke who later became his intimate friend and medical adviser. He agreed with the official verdict and even guarded the clothes of the persecutors so that they could more effectively hurl down rocks and stones on the one who had so violently accused them, though we are not told that he took any active part. From that day on a great persecution arose against the Church in Jerusalem and many disciples fled to what they hoped were safer places than the so-called holy city!

Judging from Saul's later mentions of Stephen, it would seem that the manner of his death made a greater impression than his carefully worked out defence. Luke adds a further parallel to the gospel story, "Devout men buried Stephen and made great mourning over him", reminiscent of Nicodemus and Joseph of Arimathea taking down the limp body of the dead Jesus and, with the three women and St John who had watched throughout the six hours of crucifixion, making a hurried embalming before the evening sabbath.

The trial and murder of Stephen made Saul more fanatical in his determination to crush all who believed that a crucified criminal could be the Messiah. The belief in Christ's resurrection inflamed the Sadducees who encouraged Saul to hunt out believers with their authority. The book of Acts pictures him in Jerusalem and as far afield as Damascus, in a frenzied campaign of hatred and oppression. It looks to readers like myself, in a psychological age, as if Saul had to fill his days with unceasing activity, in order to stifle the memories of Stephen's arguments and his faithful devotion to Jesus in death as in life. The question must often have arisen in his mind, "What if these followers of the Nazarene were right after all?" Unceasing activity would give no time to the rising doubts and questionings that nagged away in his mind. So Saul, "still breathing threats and murder against the disciples of the Lord went to the high priest and asked him for letters of authority to the synagogues at Damascus so that if he found any belonging to the Way, men or women, he might bring them bound to Jerusalem" (Acts 9:1–2). It was about noon as they approached Damascus (Acts 22:6), pressing on through the midday heat, when Paul fell to the ground, blinded, as he later described the experience, by a flash of light from the sky. He seemed to have no doubt that the blinding light was from heaven, for he spoke aloud, "Who are you, Lord?" His travelling companions heard a voice, perhaps Saul's voice, but saw no man. It was probably Saul who later told what was happening within himself, a voice saying, "I am Jesus, whom you are persecuting. Arise and go into the city, and you will be told what you are to do." When Saul got up from the ground, he found he could no longer see, so he had to grope for someone to lead him into Damascus. The proud persecutor, who started out with such confidence and purpose, entered the city shaken and blind, and was guided by his companions to the house of one Judas in the street called Straight (still called that today).

The small band of believers in Damascus had evidently heard rumours that this notorious persecutor was on the way. Now they knew that he had arrived and that something mysteriously unexpected had happened. One of them, Ananias, was praying about it wondering if the Risen Lord wanted him to do anything about it. To his troubled surprise he felt an inner urge to go to the house where the persecutor was said to be staying. He recognized that it was the Lord speaking, and voiced his disquiet, only to be told that God had a special purpose both to the people of Israel and to the Gentile world, and that He was at work with the stricken Saul who was now waiting for some initiative from the Lord who had spoken to him as he approached the city. So Ananias, somewhat trembling, went to Straight Street and, entering the house of Judas, was emboldened to lay his hands on Saul's head with the greeting, "*Brother* Saul". What an amazing greeting from a hesitant disciple to a would-be persecutor!

The result of all this divine operation was that Saul regained his sight, was baptized on the spot, and was persuaded to take food and stay on for some days, rejoicing in the great happening. The story was not yet quite finished, for the little band of believers, learning that fanatical Jews were plotting to kill their erstwhile collaborator, took Saul and let him down over the city wall in a basket, thus defeating the plotters watching the city gates and allowing him to hasten away to safety by night.

Luke, the Gentile doctor and gospel writer, must have written with excited joy this whole story, which spans some months and begins outside the city wall of Jerusalem, as the rocks and stones hurled down on the first Christian martyr Stephen, substantiating the conviction that the blood of the martyr is the fertile seed of the Church. Down the centuries many disciples must have felt that the commemoration of St Stephen follows most appropriately on the day after Christmas, for Stephen was the first to perceive the universal significance of the birth and incarnate life of Jesus whom Paul now firmly believed to be the Christ.

The New Life Begins

The New Testament does not tell us exactly how long Saul stayed in Damascus after his experience on the outskirts of the city. We are told that after the recovery of his sight he lost no time in going to the synagogues, claiming that the long-awaited Messiah had come in Jesus, who was also the successor that Moses had promised. It is no wonder that his preaching was denounced by extremist Jews who were also angry that the leader from Jerusalem whom they hoped would be the spearhead of their traditional cause was now giving powerful support to the heretics. They were not content to defeat his arguments, but even conspired to kill him. As we have seen, the anger was so threatening that the small Christian group decided that they must smuggle him out of the city by night.

It would seem likely that they would tell Saul of groups of believers at different places on the way back who could be told of the amazing change and provide hospitality and support. They themselves would be thankful for the amazing happening, for Saul's conviction that it was God's work, for his expressed readiness to accept suffering for his new faith, and for his insight that it had a gospel message for the whole world and for all ages – that Jesus was what in our present age we would call the Cosmic Christ.

Saul's arrival back in Jerusalem cannot be described more concisely and realistically than Luke's account in Acts 9:26–30, which Luke probably learned from Paul himself:

> And when he had come to Jerusalem he attempted to join the disciples; and they were all afraid of him, for they did not believe that he was a disciple. But Barnabas took him, and brought him to the apostles, and declared to them how on the road he had seen the Lord, who spoke to him, and how at Damascus he had preached boldly in the name of Jesus. So he went in and out among them at Jerusalem, preaching boldly in the name of the Lord. And he spoke and disputed against the Hellenists: but they were seeking to kill him. And when the brethren knew it, they brought him down to Caesarea, and sent him off to Tarsus.

One of the most interesting leaders involved in this short Jerusalem period is Barnabas, a Cypriot Jew. After he became a believer he had sold a plot of land, presumably in Jerusalem, and had handed over the proceeds to the apostles for community use (Acts 4:32–37). His original name was Joseph, but his warm kindliness had earned him the nickname Barnabas, meaning son of encouragement. He took Saul under his wing and, convinced of the reality of his conversion, introduced him to "the brethren". The same situation arose in Jerusalem as in Damascus. Saul's vigorous preaching aroused violent opposition from his former collaborators who attempted to kill him. Barnabas and his new friends hurried him down to Caesarea, the Roman headquarters, where a Roman citizen could rely on state protection, and finally put him on a ship for Tarsus.

It is good to note the role of Spirit-guided people like Barnabas in the lives of people who attained greater prominence in the Church than themselves. Barnabas made an invaluable contribution to the Kingdom which, at the right moment, produced spiritual greatness in others. On seeing the world-view of the Christians at Antioch, he called Paul to take his part in the development of a world vision and mission. He later continued his vocation of encouragement, as can be seen in the way he stood up to Paul when Paul refused to take Mark with them on the second missionary tour, Mark having gone back to Jerusalem during the first journey for some unstated reason which Paul judged as failure and desertion (Acts 13:13). The result of this sharp difference was that Paul and Barnabas parted company, Barnabas took Mark with him to Cyprus, while Paul in the company of Silas revisited the small bodies of believers in Galatia and went further afield to Europe (Acts 15:37–40).

Years later Paul tacitly admitted that he had been mistaken. In a letter which scholars think was not actually written by Paul himself but by someone later, interpreting the great apostle, we read of Paul's request to Timothy: "Do your best to come to me soon . . . Get Mark and bring him with you; for he is very useful in serving me" (2 Timothy 4:9,11). We may well think that Barnabas saved Mark for something much greater, namely the writing of the first gospel, confidently said by scholars to be based on the memories and preaching of his uncle, Peter.

Talking about his new life it seemed to Paul that his old life had vanished as completely as if he had died and had been raised to a new life. Under the guidance of Christ and controlled by the love of Christ he even changed his name from the Hebrew form "Saul" to the Roman form "Paul" (Acts 13:9). His relationship to Christ included participation in Christ's death: "We are convinced that one has died for all, therefore all have died" (2 Corinthians 5:14). In the same chapter he speaks of becoming a new creature, living in a new creation:

> From now on, therefore, we regard no one from a human point of view; even though we once regarded Christ from a human point of view, we regard him thus no longer. Therefore, if any one is in Christ, he is a new creation; the old has passed away, behold, the new has come. (2 Corinthians 5:16–17)

3

Paul the Citizen

Paul was almost as proud of his Roman citizenship as he was of his Jewish family background and religious tradition. On his final visit to Jerusalem, a riot was stirred up by hostile Jews from Asia who, having seen him in the city with an Ephesian Gentile friend, Trophimus, assumed that he had brought him into the Temple. A mob seized him and dragged him out of the Temple, intending to kill him. The whole city was in an uproar and the tribune in charge of the guardian soldiers seized Paul and took him into the barracks, away from the mob who kept shouting, "Away with him!"

Paul, speaking in Greek, asked the centurion if he might have a word with him, and, permission being granted, informed him, "I am a Jew, from Tarsus, a citizen of no mean city. I beg you to let me speak to the crowd." The centurion agreed, and Paul (now speaking in Hebrew) said, "I am a Jew, born at Tarsus, but brought up in this city under Gamaliel, educated in the strict manner of the law of our fathers, being zealous for God as all of you are."

The crowd listened in silence as Paul spoke of his vision outside Damascus and the momentous change that this experience had brought about, resulting in him becoming a disciple of Jesus. He went on to tell of his return to Jerusalem, where he continued to pray in the Temple as before, until one day he had a further vision of Jesus urging him to leave Jerusalem and go on a mission to the distant Gentiles. At the mention of this there was a further uproar, and the tribune ordered him to be bound and beaten. Paul, noticing the centurion about to carry this out, quietly asked him, "Is it lawful to scourge a Roman citizen, before being found guilty?", whereupon the tribune asked him directly, "Are you a Roman citizen?" When Paul replied that he was, the officer in surprise said, "I bought this citizenship", and was further taken aback when Paul declared, "But I was born a citizen."

It would seem that Paul on this occasion confirmed his earlier insight that the fact that he was a Roman citizen could be of great value and protection in obeying the conviction that he was meant by God to take the gospel to the world, and that if he kept his quiet trust and calm he would be protected and assured in that great purpose, in every similar dangerous situation. It wasn't the first danger he had been in. He might even have remembered the riot at Ephesus when the silversmiths saw that if this Jewish–Christian movement continued to grow, their livelihood would be threatened and fewer people would purchase their silver images of Diana, the Ephesian goddess.

Things moved very quickly, for the next day he

was brought before the Jewish Council, presided over by Ananias the high priest, who, as soon as Paul started to speak, commanded those near him to strike him on the mouth. Paul knew his Jewish law as well as his Roman, and retorted with some heat that it was contrary to the Law to order him to be struck. Once again Paul's alert presence of mind came to his aid, for he perceived that the Council was almost equally divided between Pharisees and Sadducees, the latter neither believing in spirits or angels or in life after death. Paul, born of Pharisee parents, the student of Gamaliel, boldly declared his faith both as a Jew and a disciple. The result was division and violence, and once again Paul had to be rescued by Roman power.

His opponents were not yet finished, for some extremists banded themselves together to kill him. They suggested that the hearing before the Council should be resumed, a very interesting incident that many readers of the account in Acts seem to overlook. Paul evidently had a sister living in Jerusalem, whose son somehow heard of the plot and went to the barracks to warn his uncle. Paul referred him to the tribune, who arranged that same night to send him to the Roman governor's headquarters in Caesarea, under a strong guard to protect him. Once again his citizenship came to his defence. Hearings before Felix the Governor and later his successor Festus, and finally before King Agrippa, gave Paul the opportunity to tell the story of his conversion. Here it would seem that Paul either got impatient or perhaps saw an almost unbelievable opportunity, and finally exercised his citizen's right to appeal to the Emperor. Luke concludes this period in Paul's history by reporting the personal verdict of Agrippa – "This man could have been set free if he had not appealed to Caesar."

Paul's hope of visiting Rome, mentioned in his epistle to the Romans, written before the happenings just recorded, was being fulfilled in a quite unexpected way. Later he was to describe this development as becoming an ambassador of Christ, even though it was to be an ambassador in chains (Romans 1:13; Ephesians 6:20).

The voyage to Rome was to be equally adventurous. Paul and some other prisoners were in charge of a centurion named Julius. He was a kindly man, for when the ship made an early call at Sidon he gave Paul leave, "to go to his friends and be cared for".

The rest of the journey was long so Julius and Paul had plenty of time to get to know one another better. At Myra in Lycea they changed ships and embarked in a ship from Alexandria making for Italy. Sailing on the south side of Crete, Paul with his experience as a traveller, suggested to Julius that it would be wiser to winter there, but Julius and the owner were in a hurry and decided to risk stormy weather. Before long they were in a storm that went on for days. Unable to steer, they jettisoned the cargo and the ship's gear, fearing the ship would break up and all lives be lost.

The only person to keep calm was Paul. He urged

all on board to take food and not abandon hope. He spotted, as they neared a rocky coast, that the sailors were about to take to the "lifeboat" leaving the passengers and soldiers helpless on board. Julius and Paul between them cut the ropes on the boat, so the sailors had to stay on the ship, which soon began to break up. Orders were given to those who could swim to do so, and the rest to cling to floating planks. In the end not a single life was lost.

Paul's confidence and presence of mind came from a spiritual experience during the night of a guardian "angel of the God to whom I belong and whom I worship", who urged him to have no fear, for he was being preserved to fulfil the divine purpose of witnessing to the Roman emperor, and the crew and passengers, being involved in furthering that purpose, would be saved with him. Luke's account in Acts 27 of the journey and shipwreck is a thrilling one, and in every incident Paul stands out as the hero of courage and action.

The crew, soldiers and passengers had no idea on which island they had struggled ashore. Most texts give the number of people in the party as 276, which would seem a very big number for a cargo ship, although some ancient versions put the number at 76 which would seem more likely. Even that number would be a strain for the islanders to feed, even though the first verses of Acts 28 say that "the natives showed us unusual kindness, for they kindled a fire and welcomed us all". Paul was evidently to the fore in collecting sticks, for in his bundle a viper was concealed, which fastened on to his hand. He quietly shook it off before it bit him, astonishing those watching, who expected his arm to swell up fatally. Superstition made them think that he was a murderer, whom justice would not let live. When nothing untoward happened they changed their minds and said he was a god. We may observe a similar change of opinion at Lystra (Acts 14:8–20).

Paul soon found a way of requiting the islanders' kindness, for in that part of the island lived the chief man, Publius, who had been foremost in hospitality. His elderly father was ill with dysentery, so Paul visited him and laid his hands on him with prayer, with the result that he recovered. Other people with various illnesses then came to Paul and he treated them in the same way. Throughout Acts 27 and 28, the personal pronoun "we" is used – Luke, the writer of Acts, may have been with Paul and would have used his medical skill in noticing familiar herbs.

In this way a happy, friendly three months passed, and when a ship wintering nearby was ready to sail for Rome, the whole party embarked, and were showered with gifts and provided with all they needed for the remaining journey. The picture conjured up in the reader's mind today is an idealistic one of the *Pax Romana* – the camaraderie of fellow travellers, of food ships bound for crowded cities, and no signs of racial or national prejudices.

So Paul reaches the capital of the Empire, an aim that has been in his mind since the shattering experience on the Damascus road many years earlier. He is to witness there as he did in every place he visited. The final chapter of Acts describes the climax:

> When we came into Rome, Paul was allowed to stay by himself, with the soldier that guarded him . . . And he lived there two whole years at his own expense, and welcomed all who came to him, preaching the Kingdom of God and teaching about the Lord Jesus Christ quite openly and unhindered. (Acts 28:16, 30–31)

He had reached Rome – but as a prisoner!

Two realistic and somewhat negative factors need to be kept in mind. First, in Rome Paul invited leaders of the Jewish community to come and hear what he had to say. They did so, saying, "we know this sect is everywhere spoken against", which prompted Paul to remind them of the warning of Isaiah to the people of his own time not to have closed minds, in which case he would have to concentrate on the Gentiles.

The second negative factor is the low level of moral conduct which Paul discusses in the epistles to the Romans and the people of Corinth. His travels and stays in the cities of Asia Minor and later in Europe had shown him the superstitions, low moral standards, and corruption of making greed for money the main motive of personal and corporate life. In the first chapter of Romans (verses 18–23) he makes his indictment, charging people generally of being without excuse, because from the beginning of creation God has been revealing his nature and will. He even thinks that God has abandoned them to their passions and lusts. His own words need no paraphrase:

> For the wrath of God is revealed from heaven against all ungodliness and wickedness of men who by their wickedness suppress the truth. For what can be known about God is plain to them, because God has shown it to them. Ever since the creation of the world his invisible nature, namely, his eternal power and deity, has been clearly perceived in the things that have been made. So they are without excuse; for although they knew God they did not honour him as God or give thanks to him, but they became futile in their thinking and their senseless minds were darkened. Claiming to be wise, they became fools, and exchanged the glory of the immortal God for images resembling mortal man or birds or animals or reptiles.

His general verdict on mankind is summed up in Romans 3:23, ". . . all have sinned and fall short of the glory of God". Had Paul stopped there his readers in Rome and in every generation since would be left in hopeless despair. But he goes on to speak of the divine forgiveness and redemption exhibited and made available through Christ for the whole of mankind, Gentiles as well as Jews.

Given the advantages that Paul saw and enjoyed in

being a citizen of the Roman Empire, Paul could hardly have forgotten to compare it, even at its best, with the Kingdom of God as taught by Jesus.

A key text is Romans 14:17, following his comments about the vexed question of eating meat which had been offered to idols: "The Kingdom of God does not mean food and drink but righteousness and peace and joy in the Holy Spirit". In reproving some of the Corinthians for arrogant boasting, and evidently feeling safe in Paul's absence, he asks them if when he does come do they want him to come in stern rebuke: "For the Kingdom of God does not consist of talk but in power" (1 Corinthians 4:20). He has always claimed authority directly from Christ and he will speak from the mind of Christ. There is another message implied in this text that deeds are more powerful than words, and when Paul speaks it will not consist of idle words only but in divine judgment as well. This implication is also relevant when Paul speaks of the foolishness of preaching.

We have thought widely and selectively of Paul the Roman citizen and the advantages that citizenship brought him in presenting the gospel of Christ to the world. There was one final personal advantage – execution for a Roman was by sharp, almost instantaneous beheading and not by the cruel torture of crucifixion which Peter had to undergo, and the Master before them both.

4

Paul's Gentile Friend

There are only two mentions of the name Luke in
the New Testament. In Colossians 4:10–11 Paul
mentions Aristarchus, Mark and Jesus Justus as sending their greetings to the Colossian disciples, adding,
"These are the only men of the circumcision among
my fellow workers for the Kingdom of God, and
they have been a comfort to me". Three verses later
he adds a greeting from "Luke, the beloved physician", which suggests that Luke was not a Jew but a
Gentile.

In the book of Acts there are three passages which
could be quotations from a travel diary in which the
pronoun "we" is used (16:10–17; 20:5–21;
27:1–28:16). The first of these deals with events at
Troas which Paul reached in his second missionary
journey. The writer of Acts tells of Paul's vision in
the night, possibly a dream, in which a man of
Macedonia implores him, "Come over to Macedonia and help us". Many dreams are sparked off
by something which has happened on the previous
day. In Paul's case it is conjectured that it was at
Troas that he had met Luke who was so impressed
by what Paul told him that he pressed Paul, who

was wondering what to do next, to accompany him back to Macedonia. Subconsciously he may have been brooding on this possibility and the dream decided the matter for him.

Another consideration may have occurred to Paul. The man from Europe was a doctor, and Paul had often been troubled by "a thorn in the flesh" (2 Corinthians 12:7). He prayed often and earnestly, but healing did not come. Paul may have thought that a Gentile doctor would know remedies that could alleviate his unspecified complaint, which some biblical scholars have suggested was malaria.

The problem of identifying this unnamed European is a fascinating one, and seems to rest on a process of eliminating others mentioned in the Pauline epistles. No one is named in the third gospel and the Acts. The opening verses in both those books speak of them as being addressed to, "most excellent Theophilus", one being to assure him of "the truth concerning the things of which you have been informed", and the other to speak of instructions given through the Holy Spirit after the death of Jesus to the chosen apostles over forty days giving "ample proof that he was alive" (NEB). Reading the pages of the second book we can see the apostles' faith continuing, the Risen Christ being with them and guiding them still, as he did in the gospel.

Writers from the end of the second century AD, notably Irenaeus (c.130–200 AD), Tertullian (c.160–220) and Origen (c.185–264), ascribe the third gospel and the Acts to Luke. Luke, if it was indeed he, in the short preface to the gospel, "having followed all things closely for some time past as they were delivered to us by those who from the beginning were eyewitnesses and ministers of the word", thought it good to write an orderly account for Theophilus. The other time Luke is named is in the second epistle to Timothy (4:11), where Paul in prison in Rome urges his "beloved child Timothy" to come to him soon, as except for Luke he is alone.

To learn more about the kind of person Luke was we need to study the two books which seem reasonably attributed to him. Most scholars agree that they were written some years after the death of Paul and after the destruction of Jerusalem in 70 AD. A special characteristic of the gospel is its insistence on the life, death and teaching of Christ as a message of universal salvation. It is indeed good news, about God, from God, through Christ. The writer does not lay great stress on the fulfilment of Old Testament prophecies but emphasizes our Lord's loving kindness and human understanding, for example in the parable of the prodigal son. Chapter fifteen links together three stories showing different ways of being lost and being found – the lost sheep through its own foolishness; the lost coin by accident; and the lost son through deliberate wilfulness. In each case the writer speaks of the joy in heaven over one sinner who repents being greater than its joy over those who don't need that repentance. Joy over both!

The gospel writer takes a great interest in the outcasts of society, as in the Parable of the Good

Samaritan, and the account of our Lord's stay in the home of Zacchaeus. He has an interest in prayer, shown especially in the parable of the pharisee and the taxgatherer in the Temple. His gospel has also been called the gospel of women. In his narratives of the birth and childhood of Jesus, his emphasis is on Mary of Nazareth rather than on Joseph. He has the lovely account of the visit of the boy Jesus to Jerusalem, and in the account of our Lord's last visit he records his moving lament on what he could see would be the ultimate fate of the city.

It is possible that Luke knew the mother of Jesus in her later years, and gathered from her memories details of the hidden years at Nazareth. He was a poet and may have composed what we speak of as the first canticles, the Christian psalms of the Magnificat, the Benedictus and the Nunc Dimittis.

Tradition also speaks of him as an artist, and he is the patron saint of artists, as well as of doctors and all involved in the medical profession.

Such then was the man whom we identify as Luke. He may have been the companion sent to Corinth with Titus: "With him we are sending the brother who is famous among all the churches for his preaching of the gospel; and not only that, but he has been appointed by the churches to travel with us in this gracious work which we are carrying on for the glory of God" (2 Corinthians 8:18–19). A splendid epitaph for one who accompanied Paul in his journeys and put himself at Paul's disposal.

As we study the book of Acts we learn of the

communal life of the Christians in Jerusalem, then incidents of a wider outreach such as Peter's visit to the centurion Cornelius and the baptism of him and his family, Philip's preaching in Samaria and his encounter with the Ethiopian eunuch and his baptism, and the decision of the Christians at Antioch to send out Paul and Barnabas on a wider mission which took them to Cyprus, Cilicia and Galatia, which resulted in an outspoken acceptance of universal salvation:

> For so the Lord has commanded us, saying, "I have set you to be a light for the Gentiles, that you may bring salvation to the uttermost parts of the earth". (Acts 13:47)

It is rather sad to note that it was the fanatical opposition of some Jews which drove Paul and Barnabas to this decision in the first place, but in the verse just quoted we note that in the end they recognized it as a positive and clear direction from the Lord.

Luke could only have heard from Paul the happenings on the first missionary journey and an account of the first Christian Council that met at Jerusalem to consider the question of whether Gentile believers should become Jews before receiving salvation. This would have entailed circumcision as well as baptism. The final decision was to lay upon Gentile believers no greater burdens than to be sensitive to things which were abhorrent to Jews and to live a moral life. In a letter to the troubled Christians at Antioch the Jerusalem conference recommended its decision with a letter which had as its key message the words, "For it seemed good to the Holy Spirit and to us". And it is very interesting that the conference sent their letters to Antioch by two trusted messengers, one of whom was Silas who became a partner in Paul's efforts for the universality of the gospel and its relevance to the whole of life.

Luke notes Paul's gift of perceiving in everything an opportunity to see God at work and to show by word and action the significance of the gospel. Even when the next step is not clear, and any way forward seems blocked, this gift impels him to wait upon God's guidance and wisdom. He trusted God so completely that later he could say in striking hyperbole, that even God's foolishness was wiser than man's highest wisdom.

The violent opposition seen in Paul's last visit to Jerusalem resulted in him making his defence and presenting his view of God's eternal purpose before the tribune and his officers in Jerusalem, the Jewish Council with its Pharisee and Sadducee members, Felix the Roman Governor and his successor, King Agrippa and his queen, the centurion and his guard, the crew on the voyage to Rome, and, at the end of all that, he had the opportunity of a trial before the most powerful men in the Roman Empire.

The book of Acts ends with Paul's imprisonment in Rome, but as one studies it, one gets the impression that the story is unfinished and there is more to come. Scholars have suggested that Luke intended to write a further book which for some reason he was not able to complete. The later expansion of the Church and the acceptance of his gospel through succeeding centuries makes good however the disappointment of there being no third book from Luke – all this was achieved in spite of human fallibilities and man's falling short of God's glorious love and eternal will.

5

Paul and Salvation

Paul's gospel is so simple and clear, so short in its wording, that it is easy to pass over without taking in its meaning, totality and universality. His conviction is that salvation is the free gift of God and cannot be gained by any legalism, system or form of words, or even by the highest code of moral conduct or the most rigid obedience to it.

> But God, who is rich in mercy, out of the great love with which he loved us, even when we were dead through our trespasses, made us alive together with Christ (by grace you have been saved), and raised us up with him, and made us sit with him in the heavenly places in Christ Jesus, that in the coming ages he might show the immeasurable riches of his grace in kindness towards us in Christ Jesus. For by grace you have been saved through faith; and this is not your own doing, it is the gift of God – not because of works, lest any man should boast. (Ephesians 2:4–9)

In his epistles there is emphasis on the word "all", both as regards the sinfulness and failure of all, and

God's all-inclusive love, mercy, forgiveness and grace:

> There is no distinction; since all have sinned
> and fall short of the glory of God, they are
> justified by his grace as a gift, through the
> redemption which is in Christ Jesus, whom
> God put forward as an expiation by his blood,
> to be received by faith. This was to show
> God's righteousness, because in his divine
> forbearance he had passed over former sins; it
> was to prove at the present time that he
> himself is righteous and that he justifies him
> who has faith in Jesus. (Romans 3:22–26)

Later Paul goes on to speak of God's complete
freedom to have mercy on whomever he wills, or
harden the heart of whomever he wills. Some, of
whom I am one, have difficulty in accepting the Old
Testament view that God hardened Pharaoh's heart
and inflicted plagues on the Egyptians. Such a view
would surely make God ultimately responsible for
Pharaoh's oppressive treatment of the Israelites, and
the consequent disasters. I ask myself if, in the light
of the teaching and actions of Christ, God would
harden anyone's heart. Would he not rather be ready
to soften by his love hearts already hard? I recall the
insight of a medieval rabbi who pictured God weep-
ing over his Egyptian children drowned in the Red
Sea. That rejoiced my heart as being very close to
Paul's understanding of the mind of Christ of which
he speaks in the last short sentence of I Corinthians

2:16, "For who has known the mind of the Lord so as to instruct him? But we have the mind of Christ."

Salvation for all is the eternal purpose of God, but it took many centuries for this to be perceived, until Jesus the Jew saw its universality, and was ready to die to bear witness to its truth and validity.

The epistle to the Galatians (2:16) speaks of both Jewish and Gentile sinners being "justified not by works of law but by faith in Christ". (I have omitted the definite article "the" and written the word "law" without an initial capital, to show that it was not the Torah or divine Law of which Paul was speaking. He recognized the danger of regarding its text as sacrosanct, and not going back to the Lord who gave it and who speaks through it.)

We need to be aware of a possible double meaning in the word "justify". It can bear the meaning "making just", and so carries the good news that God supplies the grace needed to bring this about. The second meaning has the implication that our statement is fully right in the sense of winning the argument. Luke, Paul's great Gentile friend, speaking of the discussion between Jesus and a scholarly scribe which drew out the Parable of the Good Samaritan, uses the word in this second sense when he says, "But he, willing to justify himself, said to Jesus, 'Who is my neighbour?'" (Luke 10:29). I quite often find myself in this situation, set on winning the argument, and therefore losing the hope of coming closer together in open and persuasive examination of the point at issue. Paul speaks more strongly in the last verse of the second chapter of Galatians, "I do not nullify the grace of God; for if justification were through law, then Christ died to no purpose".

In the epistle to the Romans Paul points out that Abraham, our forefather in the flesh, "believed in God, and it was reckoned to him as righteousness" (4:3). He also makes the point that Abraham was circumcized after this commitment of faith, and long years before the giving and acceptance of the Law at Sinai.

Paul warns his Galatian converts, even accuses them, of turning back "to the weak and beggarly elemental spirits" (the so-called gods of nature), "whose slaves you want to be once more". He voices a fear that he may have laboured in vain over them (4:8–11). In the opening of this epistle he immediately expresses his dismay, "I am astonished that you are so quickly deserting him who called you in the grace of Christ and turning to a different gospel", thus perverting the gospel of Christ. He even warns them that if an angel from heaven should preach to them a gospel contrary to that which he preached to them, they were not to be misled.

In Ephesians he is much more positive and declares that in Christ God has made known in all wisdom and insight the mystery of his will and purpose, "to set forth a plan for the fulness of time, to unite all things in him, things in heaven and things on earth" (1:9–10). Later in this epistle he expands his understanding of this great mystery or secret: "When you read this you can perceive my insight into the mystery of Christ, which was not made known to the sons of men in other generations as it has now been revealed to his holy apostles and prophets by the Spirit; that is, how the Gentiles are fellow heirs, members of the same body, and partakers of the promise in Christ Jesus through the gospel" (3:4–6).

In Colossians Paul says that believers "have put on the new nature, which is being renewed in knowledge after the image of the creator. Here, there cannot be Greek and Jew, circumcized and uncircumcized, barbarian, Scythian, slave, free man, but Christ is all, and in all" (3:9–11). The gospel is universal, for all. Discipleship overrides all distinctions of race and culture and economic status. It is interesting to note that in a similar statement in Galatians, Paul adds, "neither male or female" (3:28). I don't often see or hear that particular distinction quoted in discussions about the ministry today.

Paul shows his deep affection for his Jewish brethren and his sadness that they reject his insights into Jesus as the Messiah:

> I am speaking the truth in Christ, I am not lying; my conscience bears me witness in the Holy Spirit, that I have great sorrow and unceasing anguish in my heart. For I could wish that I myself were accursed and cut off from Christ for the sake of my brethren, my kinsmen by race. They are Israelites, and to them belong the sonship, the glory, the covenants, the giving of the law, the worship, and

the promises; to them belong the patriarchs, and of their race, according to the flesh, is the Christ. God who is over all be blessed for ever. Amen. (Romans 9:1–5)

Some idea of this sadness can be seen in the different ways in which translators have interpreted his feelings. The key verse in the above translation from the Revised Standard Version is:

I have great sorrow and unceasing anguish in my heart.

The New English Bible which so often gives the true meaning of passages, though not with the euphony of the Authorized or King James Version, has:

In my heart is great grief and unceasing sorrow. For I could even pray to be outcast from Christ myself, for the sake of my brothers and my natural kinsfolk.

J. B. Phillips in his paraphrase of the epistles has:

There is something that makes me feel very depressed, like a pain that never leaves me . . . and I have actually reached the pitch of wishing myself cut off from Christ, if it meant that they could be won for God.

The Jerusalem Bible has:

My sorrow is so great, my mental anguish so endless, I would willingly be condemned and

be cut off from Christ if it could help my
brothers of Israel, my own flesh and blood.

Even the Authorized Version, so beloved of older
Bible-lovers and many younger lovers of the gospel,
is simple and clear:

I have great heaviness and continued sorrow
in my heart. For I could even wish myself
were accursed from Christ, for my brethren,
my kinsfolk according to the flesh.

Such expressions of devotion to Christ and love for
his own people, even if they refuse to listen to his
appeal, give those of us who do listen both admiration for an identification with one whom we did not
suspect of having such deep human feeling.

Some of the rabbis in their writings and in friendly
conversation today believe that the covenant and the
Torah were offered to other nations as well as to
Israel. Only Israel accepted. I prefer to think that
Israel was the first that accepted both, and that others
would do so when they heard about God's offer and
understood it. God predestines all nations to his
salvation and love. None are excluded by Him. The
great Baptist preacher Spurgeon (1834–92), troubled
about the rigid views of many of his congregation on
election and predestination, prayed at the Metropoli-
tan Tabernacle in Southwark, one Sunday morning
in his pastoral prayer, with great earnestness: "O
God save the elect, and then elect some more!"

The great scientist and saintly Jesuit, Teilhard de

Chardin (1861–1955), who was not allowed by Vatican authority to publish any of his writings in his lifetime, wrote a whole series of books which his friends and followers published after his death. The first was one in which he expressed his devotion to Christ and his views of the environment in which Christians could live, *Le Milieu Divin* (1957; Eng. trans, Collins, 1960). It was in three short passages of the epistle to the Ephesians that Teilhard saw the cosmic ministry of Jesus the Christ.

> He (God) has made known to us the mystery of his will in all wisdom and insight, according to the purpose which He set forth in Christ as a plan for the fulness of time, to unite all things in him, things in heaven and things on earth. (1:9–10)

> He has put all things under his feet and has made him the head over all things for the Church, which is his body, the fulness of Him who fills all in all. (1:22–23)

> To me, though I am the very least of all the saints, this grace was given, to preach to the Gentiles the unsearchable riches of Christ, and to make all men see what is the plan of the mystery hidden for ages in God who created all things: that through the Church the manifold wisdom of God might now be made known to the principalities and powers in the heavenly places. This was according to the

eternal purpose which He has realized in Christ Jesus our Lord. (3:8–10)

A passage in the epistle to the Colossians confirms and expands Paul's faith in the Cosmic Christ:

He is the image of the invisible God, the first-born of all creation; for in him all things were created, in heaven and on earth, visible and invisible, whether thrones or dominions or principalities or authorities – all things were created through him and for him. He is before all things, and in him all things hold together. He is the head of the body, the church; he is the beginning, the first-born from the dead, that in everything he might be pre-eminent. For in him all the fulness of God was pleased to dwell, and through him to reconcile to himself all things, whether on earth or in heaven, making peace by the blood of his cross. (1:15–20)

Teilhard de Chardin makes another significant and central contribution to faith in Christ in his great study *The Phenomenon of Man*. He speaks of an Omega point towards which he saw everything converging, perceived through this study of the phenomenal and empirical. Other thinkers have come to the same conclusion, notably Julian Huxley, who wrote in the introduction to the English translation of *The Phenomenon of Man* (Collins, 1959):

He (Teilhard) saw that what was needed at the moment was a broad sweep and a comprehensive treatment. This is what he essays in *The Phenomenon of Man*. In my view he achieved a remarkable success, and opened up vast territories of thought to further exploration and detailed mapping . . . What is more, he has helped to define the conditions of advance, the conditions which will permit an increase of fulfilment and prevent an increase of frustration. The conditions of advance are these: global unity of mankind's noetic organization or system of awareness, but a high degree of variety within that unity; love, with goodwill and full co-operation; personal integration and internal harmony; and increasing knowledge . . . We, mankind, contain the possibilities of the earth's immense future, and can realize more and more of them on condition that we increase our knowledge and our love.

Teilhard went further than the secular thinkers who saw the same process at work, for he made a leap of faith in identifying Christ with the Omega point. In all his books Teilhard regarded Christ as the first perfected man, man as God meant him to be. He also regarded Christ as the spearhead of evolution leading humanity on to greater greatness, generating a Christ-likeness in individual believers. For many of my younger years I was puzzled by a text in John's first epistle:

Beloved, we are God's children now; it does
not yet appear what we shall be, but we know
that when He appears we shall be like Him,
for we shall see Him as He is. (3:2)

With the clarification which Teilhard's thought has
brought to this verse, I now associate what seems to
me to be an inspiring insight in what purports to be
the second epistle of Peter, where the writer,
whoever he may be, speaks of believers becoming,
"partakers of the divine nature" (1:4). He then
exhorts them:

Make every effort to supplement your faith
with virtue, and virtue with knowledge, and
knowledge with self-control, and self-control
with steadfastness, and steadfastness with godliness, and godliness with brotherly affection,
and brotherly affection with love. For if these
things are yours and abound, they keep you
from being ineffective or unfruitful in the
knowledge of our Lord Jesus Christ. For
whoever lacks these things is blind and short-
sighted and has forgotten that he was cleansed
from his old sins. Therefore, brethren, be the
more zealous to confirm your call and election,
for if you do this you will never fall; so there
will be richly provided for you an entrance
into the eternal kingdom of our Lord and
Saviour Jesus Christ. (1:5–11)

I have wondered, however, if Teilhard was right
in identifying Christ as the Omega point. Might it

not be more true to say that *God* is the Omega point, by whatever name we call Him? Further reflection suggests that there may not be as much difference between the two definitions of Omega as might seem at first apparent, for Christians see in Jesus the self-revelation or self-disclosure of God, his nature and will, in terms of human living:

> No one has ever seen God; but God's only Son, he who is nearest to the Father's heart, he has made Him known. (John 1:18 NEB)

In 1 Corinthians 3:10–13, Paul says of himself:

> According to the grace of God given to me, like a skilled master builder I laid a foundation, and another man is building upon it. Let each man take care how he builds upon it. For no other foundation can any one lay than that which is laid, which is Jesus Christ. Now if any one builds on the foundation with gold, silver, precious stones, wood, hay, straw – each man's work will become manifest; for the Day will disclose it, because it will be revealed with fire, and the fire will test what sort of work each one has done.

Teilhard takes up this vocation of Paul and his determination to build a foundation on Jesus Christ:

> . . . every man in the course of his life, must not only show himself obedient and docile. By his fidelity he must *build* – starting with

the most natural territory of his own self – a work . . . into which something enters from all the elements of the earth. *He makes his own soul* throughout all his earthly days; and at the same time he collaborates in another work . . . which infinitely transcends . . . the perspectives of his individual achievement: the completing of the world. (*Le Milieu Divin*)

Teilhard then calls us to engage in a third building activity in addition to the making of our own self and the collaboration in completing the world, namely creating the future. He speaks of a phylum of love, the central growing shoot of life, much in the same way as Isaiah pictured a branch developing from the central root of Jesse and David:

There shall come forth a shoot from the stump of Jesse, and a branch shall grow out of his roots. And the Spirit of the Lord shall rest upon him, the spirit of wisdom and understanding, the spirit of counsel and might, the spirit of knowledge and the fear of the Lord. And his delight shall be in the fear of the Lord. (Isaiah 11:1–3)

It is relevant to note that the Church has based on this its special prayer in the Confirmation Service, when those asking for it dedicate themselves to the new life as full and mature members of the corporate Body of Christ. The sevenfold gift culminating in delight will produce a hybrid of holiness clearly recognizable as coming from the God who is Spirit.

Teilhard also speaks of Christ as the spearhead of advancing humanity towards the spirituality, perfection, consummation and eternity which has always been God's purpose for it, a purpose which was only glimpsed before Christ, but perceived in all its fullness and wonder in and through him. Teilhard further speaks of the fullness mentioned in the Pauline epistles as *pleroma*, the totality, towards which each of us must bring our little contribution. Christ, in Paul's faith and Teilhard's, is the new man leading humanity on to greater greatness, as well as generating a Christ-likeness in the individual believer, in local communities of faith, and in the Church as a whole. The stages of growth perceived in Teilhard's thought are:

> vitalizing matter
> humanizing life
> unifying mankind
> spiritualizing man
> Christifying humans
> incorporating humans into the eternal.

So here we may see God's creating purpose and a programme of co-operation with the Creator.

There is much contemporary discussion going on about the function of morality. Paul is quite emphatic that no code of morality can win salvation, no code merit salvation, for we all fall short of God's will, shorter still of anything that will enhance God's name or add to his glory.

Paul makes clear that in his view morality or

ethical living does not produce salvation, but follows as a consequence:

> The fruit (or harvest) of the Spirit is love, joy, peace, patience, kindness, goodness, faithfulness, gentleness, self-control; . . . If we live by the Spirit, let us also walk by the Spirit. (Galatians 5:22–25)

Teilhard de Chardin sees that the function of morality is to build the world that God wants, to promote the growth of spirit in the earth, to develop and enhance the quality of life, and to encourage the growth of personality. He says that the moralist should be a technician and engineer of the spiritual energies of the world. He sees three principles which govern and complete our conception of goodness, holiness and perfection:

1. Good is that which makes for the growth of spirit on earth.
2. Good is everything that brings spiritual growth in the world.
3. The best is what assures the highest development to the spiritual of the earth.

Teilhard perhaps put it more simply and more clearly when he says that morality must be understood as that which liberates and develops personality, embodies love, promotes right relationships and so achieves deep and lasting happiness. It is from his deep and continuing study of Paul that he has reached this omnibus conclusion.[1]

Hans Küng sets out the essentials for the understanding and acceptance of this gift of "salvation-freedom":

1. The first and most important thing is to ensure that we do not do nothing, nor weakly acquiesce in everything that is said or done, nor give way to fatalistic thinking about the future.

2. We should not base our lives on work, career, success, or money. These cannot make life meaningful or justify our existence.

3. We must not be obsessed with achievement, but base our lives on a new foundation, a new attitude, a different awareness, and rely on something that can sustain us through success and failure, good and evil. In the midst of all realities we must place our trust unswervingly in that first and last reality which we name "God". But how can God be known?

4. Christians can know the real God in Jesus Christ. We must depend not on ourselves and our needs but on the merciful God, who expects an unswerving trust which alone can make us at peace with God and with ourselves. That alone can justify us.

5. If we bind ourselves in faith alone to the one Absolute, to the one true God, who is not identical with any finite reality, then we become free in regard to all finite values, goods, powers. We are no longer absorbed in ourselves; we can be the persons we really are and may become the persons God wills us to be.

Küng concludes with the same words with which Martin Luther ends his treatise *Concerning Christian Liberty*:

> That is true, spiritual, Christian freedom which frees the heart from all sins, laws and precepts, which surpasses all other freedoms as heaven surpasses earth. May God give us the power rightly to understand and keep it.[2]

1. See *The Human Search*, George Appleton and others (Collins, 1979).
2. See the introduction to the 1981 edition of H. Küng: *Justification* (Burns and Oates, 1964).

6

Paul and Suffering

Paul was one who suffered many hardships and sufferings in following the vocation that had come to him from the earliest days of becoming a disciple of Jesus, that he should take the gospel good news to the world. In his second letter to the Christians of Corinth he feels impelled to defend his ministry against critics. He gives an exhaustive and, as he himself admits, a somewhat boastful list of dangers faced and sufferings undergone on behalf of the gospel, which rouses both admiration and sympathy:

But whatever any one dares to boast of – I am speaking as a fool – I also dare to boast of that. Are they Hebrews? So am I. Are they Israelites? So am I. Are they descendants of Abraham? So am I. Are they servants of Christ? I am a better one – I am talking like a madman – with far greater labours, far more imprisonments, with countless beatings, and often near death. Five times I have received at the hands of the Jews the forty lashes less one. Three times I have been beaten with rods; once I was stoned. Three times I have been shipwrecked;

a night and a day I have been adrift at sea; on
frequent journeys, in danger from rivers,
danger from robbers, danger from my own
people, danger from Gentiles, danger in the
city, danger in the wilderness, danger at sea,
danger from false brethren; in toil and hard-
ship, through many a sleepless night, in
hunger and thirst, often without food, in cold
and exposure. And, apart from other things,
there is the daily pressure upon me of my
anxiety for all the churches. Who is weak, and
I am not weak? Who is made to fall, and I am
not indignant? (11:21b–29)

This passage shows not only physical suffering, but
also a heavy responsibility for the churches he has
founded and their growing congregations. He puts
himself in their struggles and weaknesses. He has
started this catalogue, wanting to show himself, his
critics and his readers, that he qualifies for an equal
recognition of apostleship with others. He knows
that he is being defensive. At the end he has forgotten
his claims and shows that he identifies himself with
the troubles of his converts, not only feeling for them
but feeling with them.

In his letter to the Romans Paul gives a more
carefully thought-out interpretation of suffering:

I consider that the sufferings of this present
time are not worth comparing with the glory
that is to be revealed to us. For the creation
waits with eager longing for the revealing of

the sons of God; for the creation was subjected to futility, not of its own will but by the will of him who subjected it in hope; because the creation itself will be set free from its bondage to decay and obtain the glorious liberty of the children of God. We know that the whole creation has been groaning in travail together until now; and not only the creation, but we ourselves, who have the first fruits of the Spirit, groan inwardly as we wait for adoption as sons, the redemption of our bodies. (8:18–23)

This somewhat lengthy quotation can be summarized in two verses, 19 and 23, though the logic and sequence of Paul's thought would seem more clear if we put the second first:

. . . and not only the creation, but we ourselves, who have the first fruits of the Spirit, groan inwardly as we wait for adoption as sons, the redemption of our bodies . . . For the creation waits with eager longing for the revealing of the sons of God.

We should also note that he concludes with a mention of his hope and belief in resurrection.

In the opening chapter of his second letter to the Corinthians Paul gives us an insight into the cost and travail of suffering, and the comfort he has received through their prayers for him:

We do not want you to be ignorant, brethren, of the affliction we experienced in Asia; for we were so utterly, unbearably crushed that we despaired of life itself. Why, we felt that we had received the sentence of death; but that was to make us rely not on ourselves but on God who raises the dead; he delivered us from so deadly a peril, and . . . he will deliver us again. You also must help us by prayer, so that many will give thanks on our behalf for the blessing granted us in answer to many prayers. (1:8–11)

The opening verses of that same second letter stress the comfort that God supplies, both in his own sufferings and those of the Christians of Corinth:

Paul, an apostle of Christ Jesus by the will of God, and Timothy our brother. To the Church of God which is at Corinth, with all the saints who are in the whole of Achaia: Grace to you and peace from God our Father and the Lord Jesus Christ. Blessed be the God and Father of our Lord Jesus Christ, the Father of mercies and God of all comfort, who comforts us in all our affliction, so that we may be able to comfort those who are in any affliction, with the comfort with which we ourselves are comforted by God. For as we share abundantly in Christ's sufferings, so through Christ we share abundantly in comfort too. If we are afflicted, it is for your comfort and salvation;

and if we are comforted, it is for your comfort, which you experience when you patiently endure the same sufferings that we suffer. Our hope for you is unshaken; for we know that as you share in our sufferings, you will also share in our comfort. (1:1–7)

Paul would seem to see two meanings to the word "comfort": the gentle, soothing of hurts, both physical and mental, and the earlier meaning of being made strong, supported and strengthened.

In his letter to the Philippians, written from prison in Rome, Paul drives home his teaching about suffering still further:

I count everything as loss because of the surpassing worth of knowing Jesus my Lord. For his sake I have suffered the loss of all things, and count them as refuse. (The King James Version has, "I count them as dung".)

He says that his hope is:

that I may know him and the power of his resurrection, and may share in his sufferings, becoming like him in his death, that if possible I (*too*) may attain the resurrection from the dead. (3:8–11)

In his letter to the Colossians, Paul advances an even more daring consideration:

Now I rejoice in my sufferings for your sake, and in my flesh I complete what is lacking in

> Christ's afflictions for the sake of his body,
> that is, the Church. (1:24)

The New English Bible has:

> It is now my happiness to suffer for you. This
> is my way of helping to complete in my poor
> human flesh, the full tale of Christ's afflictions
> still to be endured, for the sake of his body
> which is the Church.

J. B. Phillips paraphrases this as:

> It is true this moment that I am suffering on
> behalf of you who have heard the gospel, yet
> I am glad, because it gives me a chance to
> contribute my own sufferings something to
> the uncompleted pains which Christ suffers on
> behalf of his Body, the Church.

The Jerusalem Bible translates as:

> It makes me happy to suffer for you, as I am
> suffering now, and in my own body to do
> what I can to make up all that is still to be
> undergone by Christ for the sake of his body
> the Church.

There are two points to be noted in this mystifying
text. First of all to face and endure such suffering
with joy, not just to do so with "a stiff upper lip", as
many would think or say, but to do so, as it were
with a smile. I find I can't smile if the upper lip is
rigid with effort. The second point is that not only

does this suffering come for the present, but it will continue to do so as long as there is tragedy, opposition, crime, wounding and hurting. With advances in technology, there will come not only opportunities for good, but temptations to misuse it and cause worse suffering.

As I wrestle to get at the deep meaning of the verse under consideration, I remember a theology professor at Cambridge in my undergraduate days sixty-five years ago, who said, "There was a cross in the heart of God before ever there was one on Calvary". As a corollary we might add, "And there will be a cross in the sacred heart until the last erring son or daughter comes back to the waiting, open home".

The Holocaust

No complete study and meditation on suffering can omit one of the most terrible events in history, the awful crime and tragedy which is called the "holocaust". According to modern dictionaries the word means, "a great destruction or loss of life, especially by fire". A secondary definition is "a rare word for a burnt offering". Both meanings can clearly refer to Hitler's persecution of the Jews.

The seeds of this may well have been sown by the harsh treaty which followed the First World War, and by the passionate desire of Adolf Hitler and his Nazi followers to find a scapegoat for the German defeat. In his book *Mein Kampf*, written before he came to power, Hitler had selected the Jews for this role. Many Christians, including myself, read this book when it was published in an English translation with dismay, but hoped that it was no more than burning rhetoric, which would not be put into practice. But it was!

Some Jewish writers, as mentioned by Rabbi Norman Solomon in a balanced and moving lecture to the Polish Bishops' Conference in April 1988, have seen a deeper and, to Christians, a more troubling and accusing cause. Rabbi Norman writes, "It is surely unique that for little short of two thousand years one people had been singled out for constant and religiously sanctioned vilefaction through much of the 'civilized world'." He also declares, "For so long had Christians taught that Jews were a despised people, the rejectors and killers of Christ, obdurate in their adherence to a superseded faith, that European culture was saturated with this image of the Jew."

Hitler's determination was to exterminate every Jew. Not a single one was to survive, except a few that were well-hidden or overlooked. It was in the early 1940s that the word "genocide" was coined to describe this wholesale murder. We Christians have only to read some of the violent denunciations of Jews fulminated by St Chrysostom, Bishop of Constantinople (347–407 AD), whose name means "the golden-mouthed one", to be shocked to the heart.

Active persecutors or a society acquiescent to persecution by its leaders seem to be ignorant of St Paul's teaching in 2 Corinthians that God has entrusted to Christians the message and gospel of reconciliation (5:19), reconciliation with God and between humans.

Rabbi Leo Baeck, a survivor from the Holocaust, made this moving appeal to both Christians and Jews:

> When through the centuries have Judaism and Christianity looked each other full in the face? When did they frankly, honestly converse – frankly, wishing and daring to speak of the soul of the faith, the very heart of the belief; honestly, with that sympathy which is essential to human understanding?

Martin England, a Jewish historian, concludes his massive book *The Holocaust: the Jewish Tragedy*, with this grateful tribute to those who perished in the gas chambers:

> To die with dignity was a form of resistance. To resist the dehumanizing, brutalizing force of evil, to refuse to be abased to the level of animals, to live through the torment, to out-live the tormentors, these too were resistance. Merely to give witness by one's own testimony was, in the end, to contribute to a moral victory. Simply to survive was a victory of the human spirit.

We Christians with sensitive and penitent feeling can recognize that the suffering in the Holocaust was a triumph of faith. And as one who spent some years in Israel, I thank God that Jesus is being more and more recognized as a very great Jew who lived as a Jew and died as a Jew. The same could be said of Paul, his great disciple.

To those Christians, anxious not to betray our experience of God in Christ, Martin Buber (1878–1965) offers evidence that the gap between Christians and Jews is narrowing, following up Leo Baeck's plea:

> From my youth upwards I have found in Jesus my great brother. That Christianity has regarded and does regard him as God and Saviour has always appeared to me as a fact of the highest importance which for his sake and my own I must endeavour to understand . . . My own fraternally open relationship to him has grown even stronger and dearer, and today I see him more strongly and clearly than ever before.
>
> I am more than ever certain that a great place belongs to him in Israel's history of faith and that this place cannot be described in any of the usual categories.

7

Paul and the Resurrection

The new converts to Christ in Europe were very protective of Paul and like the "brethren" in Damascus smuggled him out of threatening situations and escorted him to where they and he decided should be the next place to visit. They welcomed Paul and Silas after their release in Philippi and sent them on their way to Salonika. Troublemakers soon caught up with them and even hired a mob to attack him. The brethren thereupon sent them off, again by night, to Beroea, where there was a more friendly reception with people eagerly examining the scriptures to check the arguments that Paul set before them. The troublemakers from Salonika were not long in arriving to stir up trouble there also. So the brethren conducted Paul as far as Athens, and may have introduced him to friends there. Paul sent a message back to Silas and Timothy to join him as soon as possible. We can only conjecture what thoughts went through his mind as he reached the city famed for its wisdom and philosophies. Luke's account of his stay there must have come from Paul later.

He wandered round the city to learn what he could about the people, their way of life and their interests.

He noticed that they were fairly prosperous, for many of them gathered on the Areopagus, an open space not far from the Parthenon, the great temple erected in honour of the goddess Athena. He was quick to note that they were always eager to hear and discuss any new ideas. The vital new thing in Paul's thinking was the resurrection of Jesus, both as evidence that he was the Messiah, and as God's seal of approval on his life, death and continuing activity. So a few days after his arrival he began to preach publicly about the resurrection. The common reaction was, "You bring some strange things to our ears; we wish to know therefore what these things mean" (Acts 16:20–21). Evidently they escorted him to the auditorium on Mars Hill near by for a public hearing.

He begins by expressing his dismay at the number of statues, altars and shrines of worship, with their dedicatory inscriptions. So he addresses them, "Men of Athens, I perceive that in every way you are very religious". We know that he was a fluent speaker in Greek (and Hebrew as well), so people listened. He then mentions an altar with an inscription which attracted his particular attention. The various translations in English differ as to the exact text on this altar. The AV has, "To the Unknown God"; the RSV, NEB and JB have "To an Unknown God"; J. B. Phillips paraphrases it as, "To God the Unknown". It is possible that the inscription could have been, "To God the Unknowable", with the implication that He can only be known when He reveals Himself.

Paul then declares that this is the God that he preaches, asserting that God the Creator of all, the Lord of heaven as well as earth, who gives life and breath and everything to all, cannot be confined to shrines made by humans, nor does He depend on human offerings. He has made of one blood, of one stock, all nations to occupy the whole earth, in the hope that they should not only feel after Him but find Him. The one God is near to "each one of us, for 'In him we live and move and have our being'; as some of their own poets have said, 'for we are truly his offspring'." So he urges his hearers not to think that the Deity is like any material substance, however precious, nor can He be worthily represented in human art, nor even imagined by human thought. In the past people have been ignorant of his divine nature, but God has overlooked past ignorance. Now they have no excuse, for He has revealed Himself in a chosen person, and has given us confident assurance by raising that person from the dead, by whom He will judge the whole human race.

Luke records the varying reactions to this clear and courageous speech: some laughed at the very idea of resurrection, others said they would think about it. Some, however, accepted the message and joined him in belief, notably a man named Dionysius, whom later thinkers were to be confused about, and a woman named Damaris, and others un-named. Paul, however, did not think the situation positive

enough to warrant further time in Athens for shortly
he moved to Corinth.

I can't help wondering that it was as a result of his
experience in Athens that in his first letter to the
Corinthians he realizes, humanly speaking, what
unpromising material the small Christian communities were, and what wisdom, right living and sancti-
fication they received from the Risen Christ:

> For consider your call, brethren; not many of
> you were wise according to worldly standards,
> not many were powerful, not many were of
> noble birth; but God chose what is foolish in
> the world to shame the wise, God chose what
> is weak in the world to shame the strong, God
> chose what is low and despised in the world,
> even things that are not, to bring to nothing
> things that are, so that no human being might
> boast in the presence of God. He is the source
> of your life in Christ Jesus, whom God made
> our wisdom, our righteousness and sanctifica-
> tion and redemption; therefore, as it is written,
> "Let him who boasts, boast of the Lord."
> (1:26-31)

Paul's ever-increasing conviction of the central
importance of the resurrection, can indeed be seen
throughout the whole of chapter fifteen of that same
epistle. He begins by showing how vitally important
the resurrection is to himself and his readers; their
whole faith and salvation depend on it. This becomes
clear as we learn more of his life, for he had never

met Jesus "in the flesh". His experience of Christ was in the Risen Christ. So he lists witnesses of it, individuals and groups – Peter, the twelve disciples (with Matthias in place of poor mistaken Judas who could neither forgive himself nor believe in our Lord's forgiveness), James "the Lord's brother", then another mention of all the apostles – these became aware of the momentous happening within forty-eight hours after Christ's death. He mentions too a gathering of more than five hundred brethren, probably in Galilee, quite a number of whom had "fallen asleep" before Paul's writing. I am very fond of the phrase "fallen asleep" which speaks to me of the ease of death, not in the sense in which modern mystery writers speak of "the long sleep". I like to think of a patient in hospital being given an injection before being taken into the operating theatre and later waking up in his own bed, with a kindly nurse helping to bring him round. So death is dropping asleep here and waking up there.

"Last of all", says Paul, "he appeared to me also", a late experiencer, but a witness all the same. Every time he remembers this experience, he feels conscience-stricken and penitent:

> For I am the least of the apostles, unfit to be called an apostle, because I persecuted the church of God. (15:9)

He goes on in a spirit of thankfulness:

> By the grace of God I am what I am, and his grace toward me was not in vain. (15:10)

In that grace he was able to work harder than earlier believers. It seems that in Corinth there were some who doubted the possibility of resurrection. Paul's argument is as pertinent to doubters today as it was to the uncertain disciples in Corinth. We are urged to believe in our resurrection because of Christ's:

> Now if Christ is preached as raised from the dead, how can some of you say that there is no resurrection of the dead? But if there is no resurrection of the dead, then Christ has not been raised; if Christ has not been raised, then our preaching is in vain and your faith is in vain. We are even found to be misrepresenting God, because we testified of God that he raised Christ, whom he did not raise if it is true that the dead are not raised. For if the dead are not raised, then Christ has not been raised. If Christ has not been raised, your faith is futile and you are still in your sins. Then those also who have fallen asleep in Christ have perished. If for this life only we have hoped in Christ, we are of all men most to be pitied. (15:12–19)

He then speaks of Christ as the first fruits of those who have died, reminiscent of a phrase of his in his careful epistle to the Romans, in which he speaks of Christ as the first-born of many brethren, the elder brother in God's great family (8:29). I can't think that this means that God only decided on spiritual life after physical death when Jesus was raised in the power of God, but that the eternal will was only shown forth and made clear in the resurrection of Jesus.

I was a green young priest at the time of the 1928 revision of the Book of Common Prayer, and one of the things for which I was most grateful was the new collect included for a funeral, which made it clear that the relatives and Church were reverently and affectionately disposing of the dead body, no longer the fitting instrument of the living spirit:

> O Father of all, we pray to thee for those whom we love, but see no longer. Grant them thy peace; let light perpetual shine upon them; and in thy loving wisdom and almighty power work in them the good purpose of thy perfect will; through Jesus Christ our Lord.

Paul clearly accepted the scriptural view that sin had come through man's disobedience from the first and death was a consequence. He was equally sure that Christ was man as God meant him to be, the first of a new race of men and women, who by committing themselves to him, would share and inherit his deathless life. And he looks forward to a great consummation, when Christ will offer the perfected Kingdom to God and God will be everything to every one.

He then mentions a practice that had grown up in some of the churches of being baptized on behalf of the dead, so that they too might share in the resurrection. This hope, he argues, would be hopeless if there is no resurrection, and his own efforts, notably at

Ephesus, would have been in vain. All that remains would be to live for this life only, which would amount to having no knowledge of the Eternal God.

He goes on to deal with a question which must have been asked many times when he presented what to him was the essence of the gospel of Christ, namely what kind of body will the dead have. He tries to answer this point by an analogy from nature, where a seed, which looks like a dried up kernel, has to be buried in the earth if the life within it is to germinate and grow into what God plans for it. This is an echo of the teaching of Jesus in the parables of the sower and his seed in Matthew's great chapter thirteen (the Kingdom parables) and the telling little parable in Mark 4:26–29 of the seed growing secretly.

The secret of death and life is summed up in the closing words of Paul's chapter on Christ's resurrection and ours:

> This perishable nature must put on the imperishable, and this mortal nature must put on immortality. When the perishable puts on the imperishable, and the mortal puts on immortality, then shall come to pass the saying that is written: "Death is swallowed up in victory." (1 Corinthians 15:53–54)

The saying which Paul quotes comes from Isaiah 25:8 which the prophet speaks of as spoken by the Lord:

> He will swallow up death for ever, and the Lord God will wipe away tears from all faces,

and the reproach of his people he will take away from all the earth; for the Lord has spoken.

The very next verse speaks of the joy of God's salvation:

It will be said on that day, "Lo, this is our God; we have waited for him, that he might save us. This is the Lord; we have waited for him; let us be glad and rejoice in his salvation."

I have always been grateful to Bishop Stephen Neill for showing me a manuscript in his own handwriting dealing with sin, death and forgiveness:

There is no anguish of anticipation or of fear in the death of the beasts; there should be none in the death of man. The distortion of values which sin has brought about has made this life seem immensely precious, and the loss of it the one final and irreparable disaster. Alienation from God has made it hard to believe that to fall asleep here is no more than to awaken elsewhere. The sense of guilt and unpaid debts arouses fears of strict account and retribution. If the presence of God is withdrawn, to die is to step out into an unknown and horrifying abyss.

Paul's gospel sets right this alienation, with the thought that in Christ, God was reconciling the world to Himself.

He ends this great chapter with a cry of triumph and an appeal to the original readers in Corinth and to those who read it today:

> O death, where is thy victory?
> O death, where (*now*) is thy sting?
> Therefore, my beloved brethren, be steadfast, immovable, always abounding in the work of the Lord knowing, that in the Lord your labour is not in vain. (15:55, 58)

In what is thought to be the first of all his epistles, Paul allays the anxiety of those who are worried about the fate of relatives and friends who have died:

> We would not have you ignorant, brethren, concerning those who are asleep, that you may not grieve as others do who have no hope. For since we believe that Jesus died and rose again, even so, through Jesus, God will bring with him those who have fallen asleep. (1 Thessalonians 4:13–14)

In the carefully-worded epistle to the Colossians, Paul speaks to all who have begun a new life in Christ:

> If then you have been raised from the dead with Christ, seek the things that are above, where Christ is, seated at the right hand of God. Set your minds on things that are above, not on things that are on earth. For you have died, and your life is hid with Christ in God.

When Christ who is our life appears, then you also will appear with him in glory. (3:1–4)

Paul suggests that a new kind of sight is available for us:

We look not to the things that are seen, but to the things that are unseen; for the things that are seen are transient, but the things that are unseen are eternal. (2 Corinthians 4:18)

We can experience resurrection and eternity now, when we are silent before God, with outside noises unheard and the traffic of our minds stilled, then come moments of full awareness, timeless moments no longer under the domination of space and time, a direct apprehension of reality, with a quiet peace in which times seems to stand still. At other times there is a sense of holding a bucket under a waterfall, with God pouring into our souls such immediate clarity, apprehension and intuition, that our conscious minds can only retain a fraction of what we have felt and heard.

Another prayer from the 1928 Prayer Book is appropriate and relevant to all of us who want to know how we might live the new life now:

O Heavenly Father, who in thy Son Jesus Christ, hast given us a true faith, and a sure hope; Help us, we pray thee, to live as those who believe and trust in the Communion of Saints, the forgiveness of sins, and the resurrection of life everlasting, and strengthen this faith and hope in us all the days of our life: through the love of thy Son, Jesus Christ our Saviour.

8

Solidarity in Sin and Grace

It would seem that Paul with all his understanding of
the meaning of the gospel to individuals, was also
trying to get his hearers and readers to realize its
universality. He sees a solidarity in God's creation of
humans, in God's love for us all, in his will that all
shall be saved. He also emphasizes a solidarity in sin:
"All, both Jews and Greeks, are under the power of
sin . . . All have sinned and fall short of the glory of
God" (Romans 3:9, 23). He quotes sadly Psalm 14:

> None is righteous, no not one;
> No one understands, no one seeks for God.
> All have turned aside, together they have gone
>   wrong,
> No one does good, not even one. (Romans
>   3:10–12)

Then he enlarges on this with quotations from
other psalms, clearly implying that people in his own
day are as sinful as those in the days in which the
psalmists wrote (and indeed in our own and every
age).

In the opening chapter of the epistle to the Romans

Solidarity in Sin and Grace

Paul speaks very plainly of the evils in the world, and claims that people have no excuse:

> For the wrath of God is revealed from heaven against all ungodliness and wickedness . . . For what can be known about God is plain to them because God has shown it to them . . . in the things that have been made . . . Although they knew God, they did not know Him as God or give thanks to Him, but they became futile in their thinking and their senseless minds were darkened . . . Therefore God gave them up in the lusts of their own minds . . . they worshipped and served the creature rather than the Creator. (1:18–25)

The wrath of God is mentioned in two or three other places in this epistle. Paul makes it clear that God does not get angry (as we humans tend to do) and inflict suffering and punishment on us. In Romans 1:24, as we have seen, Paul says, "God gave them up in the lusts of their hearts". If we insist on going our own way, God allows us to do so. Dr C. H. Dodd brings out the tragic consequences in his short book, *The Meaning of Paul for Today*: "The 'Wrath', then, is revealed before our eyes as the increasing horror of sin working out the hideous law of cause and effect." In an even more up-to-date expression Dodd adds: "The Wrath of God as seen in actual operation, consists in leaving human nature to stew in its own juice." An equally depressing verdict would be: "The wages of sin is real and terrible: it is moral decay and death for the race."

Christ is our Hope

Paul emphasizes the connection between deeds and consequences in his letter to the Galatians:

> Be not deceived; God is not mocked, for whatever a man sows, that he will also reap. For he who sows to his own flesh will reap corruption; but he who sows to the spirit will reap eternal life. And let us not grow weary in well doing, for in due season we shall reap if we do not lose heart. So then, as we have opportunity, let us do good to all men, and especially to those who are of the household of faith. (Galatians 6:7–10)

The household of faith has always got its eyes on the whole human race and God's eternal purpose for it, centred on his divinely inspired and perfect Son, Jesus Christ.

Paul emphasizes that there is a harvest from good sowing as well as evil, "The fruit of the Spirit is love, joy, peace, patience, kindness, goodness, faithfulness, gentleness, self-control" (Galatians 5:22) – a crop of lovely virtues, which come as a result of sowing spiritual seeds, which produce a harvest amounting to thirty, sixty, or even one hundred times greater than the seeds sown. (See Matthew 13:1–23.)

Dodd has not had his last word: "Jesus Christ, who Paul professed to follow, took no such gloomy view of human nature and its prospects. It was his first and chief care to give hope to those who seemed hopeless and to assure them of the glorious possibilities open to them in the love of the Father in heaven." Yet Dodd warns, "We cannot quote Jesus against Paul as giving an easy and cheerfully optimistic view of the actual state of humanity. On the contrary, there is enough in the teaching of Jesus to show that he too saw the society of his day, 'rushing down a steep place into the sea', with no hope of its redemption save in the sovereignty of God. Therein Paul was his true interpreter to the wider world."

In epistles other than that to the Romans, Paul brings out God's love for all and his will to save all, if they will accept that salvation. In his very first epistle Paul says: "God has not destined us for wrath, but to salvation through Jesus Christ" (1 Thessalonians 5:9). Many years and epistles later, using the symbol of being bought out of slavery, he continues: God our Saviour desires all men to be saved and to come to the knowledge of the truth. For there is one God and there is one mediator between God and men, the man Christ Jesus, who gave himself as a ransom for all, the testimony to which was borne at the proper time (1 Timothy 2:4–6).

This divine will, this hope, this salvation is meant for all and available for all without distinction of any kind. In his well-worked-out epistle to the Romans, Paul declares "God shows no partiality" (2:11). Peter is equally emphatic, using the same words as Luke reports him saying to Cornelius and his family, in his courageous visit and the surprising things that happened on that occasion. The whole chapter needs to be studied and meditated upon in depth (Acts 10). God has no favourites, there is no preferential treatment with Him.

We, living today, need to take this point seriously as we learn about people of other races, colour, language, tradition and experience. There can be no snobbishness in our contact with them, no insistence that we have the whole truth and nothing but the truth, and that no one else has any apprehension of truth.

9

Paul was Human

"We also are men of like nature with you." This was the hurried exclamation of Paul and Barnabas to the crowd at Lystra who, after the healing of a cripple, shouted excitedly that gods in the likeness of men had come among them. They even gave them names from their Greek myths – Zeus or Jupiter for Barnabas, Hermes or Mercury to Paul who was the chief spokesman, the messenger of the gods. The priest of the temple to Zeus outside the city even arrived to garland the two speakers and offer the sacrifice of a bullock. This unexpected development dismayed Paul and Barnabas and called forth an emphatic denial, rending their garments to show the extent of their dismay.

They ran hastily among the people to explain that they were bearing witness to God the Creator, who in his kindness sent the rain from heaven, ordering the seasons to produce crops to feed their bodies and bring happiness to their hearts. Paul went on to say that past generations had lived in ignorance which God had overlooked, but now had openly given this evidence of his providence and goodness. They urged them to turn from worthless things and superstitions to the living God, whose gospel they were proclaiming. Luke whose account in Acts of the doings at Lystra says that it was with great difficulty that they dissuaded the priest of Zeus and the crowd from offering the sacrifice.

The incident was not yet finished, for a few days later the troublemakers from Iconium arrived on the scene and so stirred up what must have been a bewildered crowd, who thereupon stoned Paul and dragged his limp body outside the town, believing he was dead. To the surprise of his few friends standing round Paul was comparatively unhurt and on the following day he and Barnabas went on to Derbe and preached the good news there. The little band of disciples left behind at Lystra must have felt that he was an example of human nature at its heroic best.

As one meditates on this, one cannot help seeing a second way in which Paul shared in the nature common to all humans. More heroic and with the level of greatness achieved by few, Paul was fallible like the rest of us, accepting some of the cultural ideas of his own times. This is seen clearly in his attitude to women.

> As in all the churches of the saints [a hopeful synonym for Christians] the women should keep silent in the churches. For they are not permitted to speak, but should be subordinate, even as the law says. If there is anything they desire to know, let them ask their husbands at

home, for it is shameful for a woman to speak in church. (1 Corinthians 14:33b–35)

Paul gives his view that women should also keep their heads covered, while a man ought not to do so. He goes on:

> For man was not made from woman, but woman from man. Neither was man created for woman, but woman for man. (1 Corinthians 11:8–9)

> I want you to understand that the head of a woman is her husband. (1 Corinthians 11:3)

> Wives be subject to your husbands as to the Lord. For the husband is the head of the wife as Christ is the head of the Church his body, and is himself its Saviour. As the Church is subject to Christ, so let wives be subject in everything to their husbands. (Ephesians 5:22–24)

He adds some qualifying clauses:

> Husbands love your wives, as Christ loved the Church and gave himself up for her . . . Husbands should love their wives as their own bodies . . . A man shall leave his father and mother and be joined to his wife, and the two shall become one. (Ephesians, 5:25, 28, 31)

In this spirit it would not be difficult for his final direction to be fulfilled:

Let the wife see that she respects her husband.
(Ephesians 5:33)

There was evidently an order of widows in the
Pauline churches, for whom Paul gave directions:
"Let a widow be enrolled if she is not less than sixty
years of age . . . But refuse to enrol the younger
widows; for when they grow wanton . . ." (1 Timothy 5:9–11). Yet he is not quite consistent: "Never-
theless, in the Lord woman is not independent of
man, nor man of woman; for as woman was made
from man, so man is now born of woman. And all
things are from God" (1 Corinthians 11:11–12). It
would seem that Paul does not accept the parabolic
form of the early Genesis story, and his biology is
not that of the biologists of today.

Yet women, sometimes spoken of as "leading
women", were among the first to accept the gospel.
After Paul's first preaching in Europe at Philippi,
Luke has the following report:

> One who heard us was a woman named Lydia,
> from the city of Thyatira, a seller of purple
> goods, who was a worshipper of God. The
> Lord opened her heart to give heed to what
> was said by Paul. And when she was baptized,
> with her household, she besought us saying,
> "If you have judged me to be faithful to the
> Lord, come to my house and stay." And she
> prevailed upon us. (Acts 16:14–15)

After Paul and Silas were released from prison they
went at once to Lydia's home, where the small group

of disciples, probably including the converted jailer and his family, had gathered, and having encouraged and blessed them they went on their way (16:40).

Luke further records what happened in Beroea: "Many of them therefore believed, with not a few Greek women of high standing as well as men" (17:12). After Paul's preaching at Athens, Luke also noticed that among those who joined Paul was a woman named Damaris (17:34). In his epistle to the Romans, he speaks very highly of a faithful woman colleague:

> I commend to you our sister Phoebe, a dea-
> coness of the Church at Cenchreae, that you
> may receive her in the Lord as befits the saints,
> and help her in whatever she may require from
> you, for she has been a helper of many and of
> myself as well. (16:1–2)

The Authorized Version speaks of Phoebe as a "ser-vant of the Church", while the New English Bible speaks of her as "a fellow-Christian who holds office in the congregation at Cenchreae".

Writing of two Jews, husband and wife, who had recently come from Corinth because the Emperor Claudius had ordered all Jews to leave Rome, Luke varies in putting Aquila before his wife Priscilla and putting the name of the wife first, a hint that Priscilla was of equal standing with her husband (Acts 18:2; Romans 16:3; 2 Timothy 4:19; 1 Corinthians 16:19). Paul's estimate of her quality and office was high, in spite of his general subordination of the feminine.

Questionable Optimism

Another point in which we today differ from Paul in his time is his statement in Romans 13:1-4:

> Let every person be subject to governing authorities. For there is no authority except from God, and those that exist are instituted by God. Therefore he who resists the authorities resists what God has appointed, and those who resist will incur judgment. Would you have no fear of him who is in authority? Then do what is good and receive his approval, for he is God's servant for your good.

Many of us would feel that this is altogether too optimistic about the Roman Empire, in spite of the privileges he enjoyed from being a citizen. He goes on:

> For the same reason you also pay taxes, for the authorities are ministers of God attending to this very thing. Pay all of them their dues, taxes to whom taxes are due, revenue to whom revenue is due, respect to whom respect is due, honour to whom honour is due. (Romans 13:6-7)

Most of us would have no difficulty in accepting the last two imperatives, and would acquiesce in the right to level taxes, but would find difficulty in agreeing that authorities are ministers of God, though hoping that they would want to live up to such a high ideal. Some would go as far as to refuse to pay taxes to oppressive governments, and many more claim the right to be critical of policies which ignore injustices inflicted on any deprived groups in the community.

Personal Struggles

Paul gives his readers a moving picture of his own spiritual and moral struggles in Romans 7:15–24:

> I do not understand my own actions. For I do not do what I want, but I do the very thing I hate . . . For I know that nothing good dwells within me, that is in my lower nature. I can will what is right, but I cannot do it. For I do not do the good I want, but the evil I do not want is what I do . . . For I delight in the law of God, in my inmost self, but I see in my members another law at war with the law of my mind.

He concludes: "Wretched man that I am! Who will deliver me from this body of death?" Most of us may not be able to say that we delight in the law of God as Paul could say, but we might be able to say with him that we often find ourselves doing the things that we know are wrong. If Paul had ended his self-analysis with that cry about his wretchedness, we who study him would feel as wretched and seemingly helpless as he did. Fortunately he went on further: "Thanks be to God through Jesus our Lord!" His grace is available for us. His willing death on the Cross assures us of his unlimited love and forgiveness.

Criticism

Some readers and scholars are critical when they find Paul saying that his hope is to be, "All things to all men" (1 Corinthians 9:22). This does not mean that Paul has no fixed principles and so changes his views to further his own arguments. Rather it means that he puts himself in the place of others so as to know how best to present the gospel to them. He wishes to understand them so as to be able to present arguments relevant to their situation, without going against his own convictions. He is not unprincipled, but wishes to understand the background and experience from which others speak. At the end of it all he may have to be challengingly critical, without becoming censorious or determining to win the argument, or ignoring any hint of truth or intention to do what seems to be right. Such an attitude would often be more difficult to acquire.

In his second letter to the Christians in Corinth,

Paul admits that what he is saying does not have the Lord's authority, and he recognizes that in reciprocal boasting he is acting foolishly (2 Corinthians 11:17). He concludes this meditational defence with, "If I must boast, I will boast of the things that show my weakness", having in the preceding verse shown also his identification with the weakness of others. "Who is weak, and I am not weak? Who is made to fall, and I am not indignant?" His desire for truth is shown in his willingness to be judged by God: "The God and Father of the Lord Jesus knows that I do not lie" (11:29–31). I can't help feeling that when Paul says *in this case* that what he is saying does not have the Lord's authority, it is not an isolated instance, but something that is consonant with his understanding of the mind of Christ, and therefore to be practised in every situation.

Patience and Impatience

Paul was easily provoked, in spite of what he says in 1 Corinthians 13, "love is not easily provoked". This is seen in Luke's account when the Roman tribune ordered the chief priests and council to meet and hear Paul. Right at the beginning as Paul began to speak, the high priest Ananias ordered those near him to strike him on the mouth. Paul retorted immediately, "God shall smite you, you whitewashed wall!" accusing him of acting against the Law. Members of the

Council then accused Paul of insulting the high priest, to which Paul replied that he did not know the speaker was the high priest.

Readers of John's gospel will remember Jesus in a similar situation when Annas the high priest asked him about his teaching and his disciples, hoping that he might say something incriminating. Jesus replied that he taught openly in the Temple and synagogues and that there were hearers who could give evidence of what he said. At this point one of the officers struck Jesus, who with quiet dignity questioned the right to do this – a very different reaction to that of Paul (John 18:19–24).

Paul and Mark

Paul could not have been an easy person to work with. He had been angrily critical when, on the first missionary journey with Barnabas, for some unexplained reason John Mark went back to Jerusalem from Perga (Acts 13:13). When Paul suggested to Barnabas later that they should return to the places previously visited, Barnabas agreed and wanted to take John Mark with them again, but Paul was against this. Luke writes, "And there arose a sharp contention so that they separated from each other". Barnabas took Mark with him to Cyprus, and Paul chose Silas to be his companion. One cannot help feeling that Mark's behaviour on the earlier tour was a failure on his part, and that Paul's refusal to take him again was understandable. Much later when he was in prison in Rome, Paul wrote to Timothy, "Get Mark and bring him with you; for he is very useful in serving me" (2 Timothy 4:11). The gentler treatment by Barnabas ("the son of encouragement") had resulted in Mark's rehabilitation and saved him not only to help Paul in his imprisonment, but also to write the gospel which bears his name.

Paul and Peter

The relationship between these two men was an important factor in the expansion of the Church, and in their interpretation of the divine purpose in history. Both were natural leaders, both were quick in perception and action, both believed that they were inspired by God, and both were inspired by their devotion to Jesus the Christ. In one way we may think that Peter had an advantage in having known Jesus in his human life. On the other hand Paul's knowledge of the risen life of Jesus and his significance for the world as well as the individual, is also the way in which we, as post-Pauline and post-Petrine disciples, have to experience him.

We must not forget the insight of Peter to the resurrection:

> Blessed be the God and Father of our Lord
> Jesus Christ! By his great mercy we have been

born anew to a living hope through the resurrection of Jesus Christ from the dead, and to
an inheritance which is imperishable, unde-
filed, and unfading, kept in heaven for you,
who by God's power are guarded through
faith for a salvation ready to be revealed in the
last time. (1 Peter 1:3–5)

This is followed by a most moving verse which Paul
would have appreciated had he seen it in manuscript
and which is as relevant to Christians of every
generation:

Without having seen him you love him;
though you do not now see him you believe
in him and rejoice with unutterable and exalted
joy. (1:8)

Paul, speaking of his conversion, says that he did
not go up to Jerusalem straight away but went to the
countryside around Damascus to work out the implications of what had happened. It was three years later
that he spent fifteen days with Peter. Perhaps it was
then that the two worked out a common understanding, namely that Paul had been,

entrusted with the gospel to the uncircumcized, just as Peter had been entrusted with the
gospel to the circumcized (for he who worked
through Peter for the mission to the circumcized worked through me also for the Gentiles). (Galatians 2:7–8)

Yet Paul also makes it clear that nothing had been added to what had come to him directly from the Spirit. He adds that James, the head of the Jerusalem church, and Peter and John, "reputed to be pillars", gave to him and Barnabas the right hand of fellowship and acceptance of the position summarized in his own words, quoted above.

It looks as if Paul was never quite sure about Peter, for he mentions that on an occasion when Peter came to Antioch he opposed him face to face, and accused him of weakening (Galatians 2:11). At that meeting in Antioch Paul accused Peter of trying to insist that Gentiles should live as Jews thus betraying Paul's gospel message that salvation was the free gift of God through Christ. Paul was even more troubled when he found Barnabas seemingly weakening on that central point. He was both hurt and angry on behalf of the Christians in Galatia (modern Turkey) who had come to Christ through him. The measure of his feelings can be perceived in the opening verse of chapter three: "O foolish Galatians, who has bewitched you that you should not obey the truth?" He drives home his reproach by reminding them that the crucified Christ had been set before them with such poignance and emphatic appeal. His conclusion is that for all who have put on Christ, "There can be neither Jew nor Greek, neither slave nor free, neither male nor female, for you are all one in Christ Jesus" (Galatians 3:27–28). We are not told what was the consequence of this passionate outburst either at Antioch or when the letter was read to the Galatian waverers, but it would seem that Paul gained his point. One would however rather like to know Peter's version of what took place.

Another occasion when Paul could hardly restrain his anger was when rebuking the Christians in Corinth for going to law when they had differences which ought to have been settled within the Christian community:

> When one of you has a grievance against a brother, does he dare go to law before the unrighteous instead of the saints? Do you not know that the saints will judge the world? And if the world is to be judged by you, are you incompetent to try trivial cases? Do you not know that we are to judge angels? How much more, matters pertaining to this life! If then you have such cases, why do you lay them before those who are least esteemed by the church? I say this to your shame. Can it be that there is no man among you wise enough to decide between members of the brotherhood, but brother goes to law against brother, and that before unbelievers? To have lawsuits at all with one another is defeat for you. Why not rather suffer wrong? Why not rather be defrauded? But you yourselves wrong and defraud, and that even your own brethren. (1 Corinthians 6:1–8)

His strength of feeling is seen in the language he uses: "I say this to your shame".

Paul when he wrote this stern rebuke did not have any of the gospels before him in writing. Had he done so, he would have had dominical authority for his judgment and action, though he might have felt troubled about his anger:

> If your brother sins against you, go and tell him his fault between you and him alone. If he listens to you, you have gained your brother. But if he does not listen, take one or two others along with you, that every word may be confirmed by the evidence of two or three witnesses. If he refuses to listen to them, tell it to the church; and if he refuses to listen even to the church, let him be to you as a Gentile and a tax-collector. (Matthew 18:15–17)

10

Paul and Love

Few of us who know something about Paul would claim that the characteristic that strikes us first and foremost was that he was a great exponent and authority on love, or that he could be described as both loving and loveable. Yet the passage that we hear most often read or quoted is the short chapter thirteen of his first letter to the Christians of Corinth, often entitled "A hymn of love". This passage alone should suggest that we ought to reconsider our earlier estimates of him.

In 1736 Alexander Cruden began to put together his bible concordance. It must have kept him well occupied throughout the eighteen months that it took to complete, before he presented a first copy to Queen Caroline, the wife of King George the Second. It was a task for which he was well qualified by long study of the scriptures and a habit of tracing words through both Testaments for his own interest and edification. The entry for the word "love", and its cognates, occupies six closely-printed columns, each with an average of seventy references, some of which are multiple. To pick out the references in the epistles attributed to Paul is a further exercise of careful perception. From the study of these references the student has to collect those which add to Paul's understanding of love and our own.

The one verse that might be thought of as the most meaningful is Romans 5:5: "God's love has been poured into our hearts through the Holy Spirit which has been given to us". Study of it and meditation on it asserts that God is loving, the Source and Origin of love, and that there is a generous and continuous outpouring of this divine gift, of which we are made aware through the indwelling of the Holy Spirit in the deepest level of our human personality. We might go further and say that it is only when we in some degree experience the Spirit within us and open ourselves to his inspiration, guidance and encouragement that we begin to experience true love.

In chapter twelve of 1 Corinthians Paul speaks of the varying spiritual gifts to the Church through Christ Jesus – wisdom and knowledge, expressed in speech and preaching; faith and trust; speaking in ecstatic tongues and the interpretation of them; discernment between good and evil; and leadership and organization – all comprising different forms of ministry. At the end of this catalogue, Paul says, "I will show you a still more excellent way". Then follow his insights on love.

When we come to study and meditate on the thirteen verses of the following chapter, we can identify three clear sections. The first four verses speak of all these varying gifts being weak and ineffective unless motivated by love and carried out in love. Without love they are like a booming gong or crashing cymbal. Without love I achieve nothing. The next three verses speak of the practice of love, piling sixteen verbs on top of one another. The version in the Jerusalem Bible pierces into my conscience and challenges my behaviour:

> Love is always patient and kind; it is never jealous; love is never boastful or conceited; it is never rude or selfish; it does not take offence, and is not resentful. Love takes no pleasure in other people's sins but delights in the truth; it is always ready to excuse, to trust, to hope, and to endure whatever comes.

The third section speaks of the enduring quality of love. All the other gifts will ultimately come to an end or be no longer necessary, but love never ends, never fails. It can outlast anything. Our present knowledge is imperfect and partial; when the perfect is come my knowledge will be whole like God's knowledge of me. Now my knowledge is like the blurred reflection in the kind of metal mirror used in Paul's time. Paul concludes his effort to describe love, human and divine, with the statement that there are three things that last for ever, three eternal verities – faith-trust, hope and love – but the greatest of these is love. All of the modern translations of this amazing chapter set before the reader an ideal to think about, pray about and progressively imitate.

In the great prayer for the disciples at Ephesus and the churches around it, the writer, whether Paul or inspired by Paul, prays that they may be rooted and grounded in love, and grasp the breadth and length and height and depth of the love of Christ which surpasses knowledge. He ends his prayer with a moving doxology:

> Now to Him who by the power at work within us is able to do far more abundantly than all that we ask or think, to Him be glory in the church and in Christ Jesus to all generations, for ever and ever. Amen (3:20–21).

All the Pauline Epistles have some mention of love in them. 1 Thessalonians, the first to be written, breathes a spirit of affection:

> But we were gentle among you, like a nurse taking care of her children. So, being affectionately desirous of you, we were ready to share with you not only the gospel of God but also our own selves, because you had become very dear to us. (2:7–8)

> For you are our glory and joy (2:20)

> But now that Timothy has come to us from you, and has brought us the good news of your faith and love and reported that you always remember us kindly and long to see us, as we long to see you . . . (3:6)

His prayer for them is that "the Lord [may] make you increase and abound in love to one another and to all men, as we do to you" (3:12). Their defence against attack should be "the breastplate of faith and love" (5:8). They must show their affection to one another and "Greet all the brethren with a holy kiss" (5:26).

In his second letter to his disciples at Salonika, he is thankful to God that they are growing in love.

> We are bound to give thanks to God always for you, brethren, as is fitting, because your faith is growing abundantly, and the love of every one of you for one another is increasing. (1:3)

The "we" indicates that he associated himself with Timothy to whom he dictates both letters and also Silvanus who is with them. He continues to pray for them, "May the Lord direct your hearts to the love of God and to the steadfastness of Christ" (3:5).

In the letter to the "saints" in Philippi (the word indicating not so much achievement but commitment and dedication), Paul shows the same personal affection:

> So if there is any encouragement in Christ, any incentive of love, any participation in the Spirit, any affection and sympathy, complete my joy by being of the same mind, having the same love, being in full accord and of one mind. (2:1–2)

He gives an even more affectionate exhortation:

Therefore, my brethren, whom I love and long for, my joy and crown, stand firm thus in the Lord, my beloved. (4:1)

He is grateful for their concern:

I rejoice in the Lord greatly that now at length you have revived your concern for me; you were indeed concerned for me, but you had no opportunity . . . Yet it was kind of you to share my trouble. (4:10, 14).

In his epistle to the Christians in Rome, the detailed setting out of his theological thinking about salvation, he declares the unlimited nature of God's forgiveness and love:

While we were still weak, at the right time Christ died for the ungodly. Why, one will hardly die for a righteous man – though perhaps for a good man one will dare even to die. But God shows his love for us in that while we were yet sinners Christ died for us. (5:6–8)

Our love must be genuine, not just pretentious piety:

Let love be genuine; hate what is evil, hold fast to what is good; love one another with brotherly affection; outdo one another in showing honour. (12:9–10)

He gives us a summary of neighbourly duty:

Love does no wrong to a neighbour; therefore love is the fulfilling of the law. (13:10)

Owe no one anything, except to love one another; for he who loves his neighbour has fulfilled the law. (13:8)

It is in chapter eight, in which he speaks of the liberation that Christ won for us, that most Christians, however little they may know of Paul, find great comfort and encouragement. In J. B. Phillips' translation:

Who can separate us from the love of Christ? Can trouble, pain or persecution? Can lack of clothes and food, danger to life and limb, the threat of force of arms?

He answers his own questions:

No, in all these things we win an overwhelming victory through him who has proved his love for us. I have become absolutely convinced that neither death nor life, neither messenger of Heaven nor monarch of earth, nor what happens today nor what may happen tomorrow, neither a power from on high nor a power from below, nor anything else in God's whole world has any power to separate us from the love of God in Christ Jesus our Lord! (8:35, 37–39)

In the epistle to the Ephesians, Paul, or someone writing in a Pauline spirit, speaks of God's eternal plan in a heart-warming paragraph:

Blessed be the God and Father of our Lord
Jesus Christ, who has blessed us in Christ with
every spiritual blessing in the heavenly places,
even as he chose us in him before the foundation of the world, that we should be holy and
blameless before him. He destined us in love
to be his sons through Jesus Christ, according
to the purpose of his will, to the praise of his
glorious grace which he freely bestowed on us
in the Beloved. (1:3–6)

In his letter to the Christians in Galatia (modern
Turkey), Paul lists the varied virtues that make up
the harvest of the Spirit:

The fruit of the Spirit is love, joy, peace,
patience, kindness, goodness, faithfulness,
gentleness, self-control. (5:22–23)

The ninth fruit in this harvest needs to be noted by
those of us who immediately leap to our self-defence,
or are quick on the trigger when attacked by provoc-
ative action or criticism.

In the short letter to Philemon, a slave-owner,
when he sends back Onesimus, a runaway, Paul
addresses Philemon as "our beloved fellow-worker
and Apphia our sister" in whose house the local
Christian community is accustomed to meet, and
commends Onesimus as "my child, whose father I
have become in my imprisonment, whom I am
sending back to you, sending my very heart, no
longer as a slave, but more than a slave, as a beloved

brother". One cannot help feeling that if Christians had taken more seriously this delightful little letter, the emancipation of the slaves and the abolition of the slave trade might have come about centuries earlier than they did.

Let this long musing on Paul's understanding of divine and human love conclude with two short texts from his second letter to the Christians at Corinth:

> For the love of Christ controls us. (5:14)

The Authorized Version has, "constrains us", which to many people conveys the idea of restraint, which is right in the sense of warning us against non-loving attitudes and behaviour. Any comments about the final words of the same epistle would blur its impression:

> The grace of our Lord Jesus Christ, and the love of God, and the fellowship of the Holy Spirit be with you all. (13:14)

Amen! Amen!

11

Paul and the Church

Paul has a great love for those whom he has brought to Christ:

> We were gentle among you, like a nurse taking care of her children. So being affectionately desirous of you, we were ready to share with you not only the gospel of God but also our own selves, because you had become very dear to us. (1 Thessalonians 2:7–8)

When rebuking the Christians in Galatia for being led away by false teachers, he describes them as, "My little children, with whom I am again in travail until Christ be formed in you" (4:19). In the epistle to the Colossians he says that his purpose is:

> to warn every man and teach every man in all wisdom, that we may present every man mature in Christ. For this I toil, striving with all the energy which he mightily inspires within me. (1:28–29)

A few verses later he urges them:

> As therefore you received Christ Jesus the Lord, so live in him, rooted and built up in

him and established in the faith, just as you
were taught, abounding in thanksgiving.
(2:6–7)

In the letter to the Philippians for whom he had a
great affection, he writes:

Therefore, my brethren whom I love and long
for, my joy and my crown, stand firm in the
Lord, my beloved. (4:1)

We must not forget his love for Philemon, a slave
owner in Colosse and Onesimus a runaway slave
who had become a disciple as a result of coming to
know Paul in his first imprisonment. To the first he
appeals, "Refresh my heart in Christ", and of the
slave he writes, "I am sending him back to you,
sending my very heart". In Christ through Paul they
enter into a new relationship as beloved brothers
(verses 10, 12, 16). In most of his letters Paul names
disciples, women and men, to whom he sends personal greetings, eager to hear of the spiritual progress
of each.

In his farewell to the elders of the church of
Ephesus whom he had called to meet him from
Miletus on his third missionary journey, when he
was hurrying back to Jerusalem in time for the
festival of Pentecost, Paul reminds them of his life
among them. The whole speech as recorded by Luke
in Acts 20:17–35 reveals his pastoral love, his unfail-
ing sense of mission to both Jews and non-Jews, his
devotion to Christ, and his expectation of trouble

when he gets back to Jerusalem. It needs not just to be read, but to be studied at length and meditated upon for the light it sheds on mission and pastoral care today:

And from Miletus he sent to Ephesus and called to him the elders of the church. And when they came to him, he said to them: "You yourselves know how I lived among you all the time from the first day that I set foot in Asia, serving the Lord with all humility and with tears and with trials which befell me through the plots of the Jews; how I did not shrink from declaring to you anything that was profitable, and teaching you in public and from house to house, testifying both to Jews and to Greeks of repentance to God and of faith in our Lord Jesus Christ. And now, behold, I am going to Jerusalem, bound in the Spirit, not knowing what shall befall me there; except that the Holy Spirit testifies to me in every city that imprisonment and afflictions await me. But I do not account my life of any value nor as precious to myself, if only I may accomplish my course and the ministry which I received from the Lord Jesus, to testify to the gospel of the grace of God. And now, behold, I know that all you among whom I have gone preaching the kingdom will see my face no more. Therefore I testify to you this day that I am innocent of the blood of all of you, for I did not shrink from declaring to you the whole counsel of God. Take heed to yourselves and to all the flock, in which the Holy Spirit has made you overseers, to care for the church of God, which he obtained with the blood of his own Son. I know that after my departure fierce wolves will come in among you, not sparing the flock; and from among your own selves will arise men speaking perverse things, to draw away the disciples after them. Therefore be alert, remembering that for three years I did not cease night or day to admonish every one with tears. And now I commend you to God and to the word of his grace, which is able to build you up and to give you the inheritance among all those who are sanctified. I coveted no one's silver or gold or apparel. You yourselves know that these hands ministered to my necessities, and to those who were with me. In all things I have shown you that by so toiling one must help the weak, remembering the words of the Lord Jesus, how he said 'It is more blessed to give than to receive'." (Acts 20:17–35)

The reciprocal love of the elders called together is shown in Luke's moving paragraph of the effect on these fellow-workers:

And when he had spoken thus, he knelt down and prayed with them all. And they all wept and embraced Paul and kissed him, sorrowing most of all because of the words he had spoken, that they should see his face no more. And they brought him to the ship. (Acts 20:36–38)

Paul has earlier spoken of the Church as Christ's corporate body:

Now you are the body of Christ and individually members of it. (1 Corinthians 12:27)

This verse sums up what Paul has said earlier in the same chapter:

For just as the body is one and has many members, and all the members of the body though many, are one body, so it is with Christ. For by one Spirit we were all baptized into one body – Jews or Greeks, slaves or free – and all were made to drink of one Spirit. (12:12–13)

In the passage between these two quotations he enlarges on the similarity between the human body and the body of Christ, a passage which we today can study more fully and meditate upon more deeply for its relevance to ourselves and to the congregations of which we are members.

The epistle just quoted is the main source for Paul's views and teaching about the Church. In its opening chapter he appeals to his readers to be united in mind and judgment. He deplores quarrelling among them:

It has been reported to me . . . that there is quarreling among you, my brethren. What I mean is that each one of you says, "I belong to Paul", or "I belong to Cephas", or "I belong to Christ". Is Christ divided? Was Paul crucified for you? Or were you baptized in the name of Paul? I am thankful that I baptized none of you except Crispus and Gaius; lest any one should say that you were baptized in my name. (1:12–15)

Chapter twelve contains Paul's own insights into the meaning of the Church and his own understanding of the nature of its members:

Now you are the body of Christ and individually members of it. (12:27)

For just as the body is one and has many members, and all the members of the body, though many, are one body, so it is with Christ. For by one Spirit we were all baptized into one body – Jews or Greeks, slaves or free – and were made to drink of the same Spirit. (12:12–13)

He goes on to talk at length of how the human body consists of many members (eye, ear, hands, feet, internal organs etc) which work together for the well-being of the whole body, without discord or rivalry. When one limb or organ suffers pain, the whole body is weakened. So it should be in Christ's body the Church, everyone is a necessary part and has his or her place in it. Verse twenty-eight lists some of the gifts and functions which God has provided – apostles or messengers, prophets or inspired preachers, teachers, miracle workers with supernatural powers, healers with ability to cure the sick, helpers and assistants, administrators and managers, some with the gift of ecstatic utterances. Paul emphasizes that not all have the same gift and that no one has all the qualities he has listed. He ends this penetrating chapter by urging his readers to set their hearts on the best spiritual gifts, and then says that he will show them even, "a more excellent Way" (12:31). As the 20th century New Testament puts it: "A way beyond all comparison the best. That incomparable way is the way of love.

In the epistle to the church in Ephesus and the cities clustering round it, Paul in prison at Rome, speaks of a God-given unity:

> There is one body and one Spirit, just as you were called to the one hope that belongs to your call, one Lord, one faith, one baptism, one God and Father of us all, who is above all and through all and in all. (4:4–6)

In the first three verses of that same chapter Paul speaks of the kind of life which all members of the Church should lead which will follow if his teaching on the Church is put into practice:

> I therefore, a prisoner for the Lord, beg you to lead a life worthy of the calling to which

you have been called, with all lowliness and
meekness, with patience, forbearing one
another in love, eager to maintain the unity of
the Spirit in the bond of peace. (4:1–3)

Paul in Romans says much the same thing about the
spirit of the Kingdom:

The Kingdom of God is righteousness and
peace and joy in the Holy Spirit . . . Let us
then make for peace and for mutual up-build-
ing. (14:17, 19)

In the letter to the Philippians Paul warns sadly
against those who live as enemies of the cross of
Christ, whose appetites are their god, whose minds
are set on earthly things, and so are heading for
destruction. Then he adds:

But our commonwealth is in heaven, and from
it we await a Saviour, the Lord Jesus Christ,
who will change our lowly body to be like his
glorious body, by the power which enables
him to subject all things to himself. (3:20–21)

C. H. Dodd, the great New Testament scholar,
describes this Divine Commonwealth in an inspired
paragraph:

It is a community of loving persons, who bear
one another's burdens, who seek to build up
one another in love, who have the same
thoughts in relation to one another in their
communion with Christ. It is all this because

> it is the living embodiment of Christ's own
> Spirit . . . The Divine Commonwealth has
> transcended the great division of men . . . it is
> on the way to comprehending the whole race.
> Short of that its development can never stop.
> This is the revealing of the children of God for
> which the whole creation is waiting.

Several other scholars follow Dodd's use of the title, "Divine Commonwealth" for the Church. Others use "citizenship", or "colony of heaven", or "the state of which we are citizens is in heaven".

Addressing the Gentile readers of his epistle to the Ephesians, Paul reminds them that at one time they were:

> separated from Christ, alienated from the
> commonwealth of Israel, and strangers to the
> covenants of promise, having no hope and
> without God in the world. (2:12)

This is the only other place in which the Revised Standard Version uses the word "commonwealth". It is an ideal which Israel never reached, any more than the British Commonwealth does. But the latter has moved forward from "empire", and does count among its members others than those of British race.

In the same sense, "One, holy, Catholic and Apostolic Church", or "Holy Mother Church" is the goal towards which all branches and all individual members should pray and strive. Those two perfections are certainly the mind of Christ and the eternal purpose of God.

12

Paul and Inter-Church Aid

After Barnabas had brought back Saul from Tarsus to Antioch, some preachers arrived from Jerusalem. One, named Agabus, foretold that there would be a widespread famine. His knowledge of the world couldn't be anything like our knowledge of the world today, but he felt a burden on his heart to rouse a deep Christian concern about it. Luke, the writer of the book of the Acts, records this incident:

> Now in these days prophets came down from Jerusalem to Antioch. And one of them named Agabus stood up and foretold by the Spirit that there would be a great famine over all the world; and this took place in the days of Claudius. And the disciples determined, every one according to his ability, to send relief to the brethren who lived in Judea; and they did so, sending it to the elders by the hand of Barnabas and Saul. (11:27–30)

By the time Paul wrote his epistle to the Romans, the charitable initiative at Antioch had become an operation in which all the churches founded by Paul joined:

At present, however, I am going to Jerusalem with aid for the saints. For Macedonia and Achaia have been pleased to make some contribution for the poor among the saints at Jerusalem; they were pleased to do it, and indeed they are in debt to them, for if the Gentiles have come to share in their spiritual blessings, they ought also to be of service to them in material blessings. When therefore I have completed this, and have delivered to them what has been raised, I shall go on by way of you to Spain; and I know that when I come to you I shall come in the fulness of the blessing of Christ. (Romans 15:26–29)

It may be that Paul had in mind this collection when he concluded what he feared might be his last visit to the elders of the churches around Ephesus whom he had called to meet him at Miletus:

In all things I have shown you that by so toiling one must help the weak, remembering the words of the Lord Jesus, how he said, "It is more blessed to give than to receive". (Acts 20:35)

The whole of his farewell speech is a reminder of the spiritual principles on which he had based his ministry, and deserves much more detailed study than this summary (Acts 20: 17–37).

In his second letter to the Christians of Corinth, Paul speaks of Titus and Luke whom he is sending to join in this gracious work:

Thanks be to God who puts the same earnest care for you into the heart of Titus. For he not only accepted our appeal, but being himself very earnest he is going to you of his own accord. With him we are sending the brother who is famous among all the churches for his preaching of the gospel; and not only that, but he has been appointed by the churches to travel with us in this gracious work which we are carrying on, for the glory of the Lord and to show our good will. We intend that no one should blame us about this liberal gift which we are administering, for we aim at what is honourable not only in the Lord's sight, but also in the sight of men. (8:16–21)

The first five verses of the same chapter end with the guiding and inspiring principle which should govern all our actions:

We want you to know, brethren, about the grace of God which has been shown to the churches of Macedonia, for in a severe test of affliction, their abundance of joy and their extreme poverty have overflowed in a wealth of liberality on their part. For they gave according to their means, of their own free will, begging us earnestly for the favour of taking part in the relief of the saints – and this, not as we expected, but first they gave themselves to the Lord and to us by the will of God. (8:1–5)

Paul goes on to remind them of our Lord's example and urges them to complete what they had embarked on in the previous year:

> You know the grace of our Lord Jesus Christ, that though he was rich, yet for your sake he became poor, so that by his poverty you might become rich. And in this matter I give my advice: it is best for you now to complete what a year ago you began not only to do but to desire, so that your readiness in desiring it may be matched by your completing it out of what you have. For if the readiness is there, it is acceptable according to what a man has, not according to what he has not. I do not mean that others should be eased and you burdened, but that as a matter of equality your abundance at the present time should supply their want. (8:9–14)

The whole of chapter nine of this second letter is relevant to the matter of inter-church aid. Paul speaks with appreciation of the readiness of the local church to engage in this collection and of his hope that they will complete the task they have undertaken (1–5). He wants it to be a willing and generous task, assures them that "God loves a cheerful giver" and that they will be enriched by God for their generosity which is inspired by God's surpassing grace and his inexpressible generosity. Chapters eight and nine form a basis for study, meditation and practice which a whole Lent's study

will not exhaust. Bishop Azariah of Domakal was
never tired of commending them as a means of
church support and wider Christian love.

We should not overlook the wise and practical
suggestions which Paul gave the Christians of Corinth in his first letter:

> Now concerning the contribution for the
> saints: as I directed the churches of Galatia, so
> you also are to do. On the first day of every
> week, each of you is to put something aside
> and store it up, as he may prosper, so that
> contributions need not be made when I come.
> And when I arrive, I will send those whom
> you accredit by letter to carry your gift to
> Jerusalem. If it seems advisable that I should
> go also, they will accompany me. (16:1–4)

A leading agency for contemporary inter-church
aid has drawn up the following guidelines:

> Work where injustices are being done to the
> world's poorest people.
>
> Help those who simply because they are very
> poor are treated as if they had no rights at
> all.
>
> Help women who are the worst off of the
> world's poor to learn vital new skills like
> health and farming.
>
> Help those who are denied the right to their
> own land and a share in its water, a right to
> fair prices for crops when they can grow them

and a right to the knowledge that can help
them to become self-sufficient.

The poor must have a share in the world's good
things.

Administrative costs should be kept to a maximum of ten per cent.

All these objectives could be realized if there was
peace between the nations, for the money saved in
defence and armaments would be available for the
hungry, the sick and the poor.

The Stockholm Institute of Peace Studies tells us
that global military spending amounts to 400,000
million dollars every year, twice as much as on health
and half as much again as on education.

750 million people in the world are badly under-
nourished.

3000 million people do not yet get pure drinking
water.

700 million adults cannot read or write and so
are unable to get a better life.

250 million children under 14 do not attend
school.

300 million people live in shanty towns and
slums.

Inflation, fortunately coming down, still
increases costs of remedial measures.

The Stockholm Institute also informs us that a five
per cent reduction in the armaments budgets could

take care of all the above needs, roughly what is spent in six weeks on military expenditure.

The United Nations Organization tells us that if every country, rich or poor, gave 0.7 of 1% of its Gross National Budget, world poverty could be banished in a generation. Seven-tenths of one per cent! The latest figures I have heard tell us that the average giving amounts to 0.37 of 1%. The Scandinavian countries reach the ideal of 0.7 of 1%. The UK is 0.34 of 1%!

Another distressing figure is that 100 million people have been killed in war during this present century. We should be ashamed of ever using the letters AD for each year – "Anno Domini" – the year of the Lord.

No prolonged study or meditation should end without prayers that would enlist us in the struggle for peace and justice in the world. I have found the following prayers imperative in my own practice of prayer, especially when I follow each petition with a silence, in which the Spirit of God can direct me as to personal response:

> Hasten the time, O Lord,
> when none of us shall live in contentment
> knowing that others have need.
> Inspire in us and in people of all nations
> the desire for social justice,
> that the hungry may be fed,
> the homeless welcomed, the sick healed,
> and a just order established in the world,

according to thy gracious will
made known in Jesus Christ, our Lord.

★ ★ ★

O God, I pray
for bread for the hungry,
homes for the homeless,
peace for the fearful,
healing for the sick,
love for the hard of heart,
life for the departed
and Christ for all.

★ ★ ★

O God, I gaze in wonder at thy creative love,
at thy seeking for people everywhere and their
search for thee, showing thyself in ways they
can understand. Help me to learn more of thee
from the experience of other communities of
faith, and so to live and love that others may
learn to share what I have found of thee in
Jesus Christ. Open my eyes, enlighten my
mind, enlarge my heart, and grant that my
own expression of thee in life and word may
come closer to thy eternal truth and love. O
God, my God, God of all.

★ ★ ★

Give, O Lord, to all who till the ground
wisdom to understand thy laws,
and to co-operate with thy wise ordering of

the world;
and grant that the bountiful fruits of the earth
may not be hoarded by the selfish
or squandered by the foolish,
but that all who work may share abundantly
in the harvest of the soil;
through Jesus Christ our Lord.

* * *

Almighty God, who fillest the earth with thy riches
for the use of all thy children,
have regard, we pray thee, to the impoverishment
of the nations;
and on all who are in authority
bestow thy gifts of wisdom and goodwill,
that being lifted above self-regard,
they may establish a new order,
wherein the needs of all men shall be supplied;
through Jesus Christ our Lord.

(*SCM Book of Prayers for Schools*)

* * *

O God, who has bound us together in this bundle of life, give us grace to understand how our lives depend upon the courage, the industry, the honesty, the integrity of our fellow men; that we may be mindful of their needs, grateful for their faithfulness, and faithful in our responsibilities to them; through Jesus Christ our Lord.

(*Reinhold Niebuhr*)

* * *

Lord Jesus Christ,
alive and at large in the world,
help me to follow and find you there today
in the places where I work,
meet people,
spend money
and make plans.
Take me as a disciple of your kingdom,
to see through your eyes
and hear the questions you are asking,
to welcome all with your trust and truth,
and to change the things that contradict God's love
by the power of your cross
and the freedom of your Spirit.

(*Bishop John Taylor*)

* * *

And a last one, which I only came across a few days ago:

Give us, Father, a vision of our world as Your
love would make it –
A world where the weak are protected, and none go
hungry or poor;
A world where the benefits of civilized life are
shared, and everyone can enjoy them;
A world where different nations, races and
cultures live with tolerance and mutual
respect;

A world where peace is built with justice, and
justice is guided by love;
And give us the courage and inspiration to build
it, through Jesus Christ our Lord. Amen.

(Oxford Diocesan Stewardship Council and
1% Working Group)

13

Paul the Prisoner

Paul had had plenty of experience of being in prison before the long stretch of imprisonment which began after the Jerusalem riot, continued on the journey to Rome, and after arrival there. On his second missionary journey he, with Silas, had been arrested, imprisoned, beaten and put in the stocks in Philippi, accused of disturbing the city and advocating "customs which it is not lawful for us Romans to accept or practise". At midnight he and Silas in spite of their pain and discomfort were singing and praying to God. The other prisoners were listening. Suddenly an earthquake shook the door open – the chief jailer, fearing he would be responsible for escapes, was about to kill himself, when Paul called out loudly, "Do not harm yourself, we are all here!" At that the jailer took them to his own house and washed their wounds, listened to Paul's message about Jesus and was baptized with all his family. Altogether the happenings of that night were quite unexpected and surprising.

The next day the magistrates sent the police with instructions to let Paul and Silas go quietly, which rather riled Paul, who complained with justice:

"They have beaten us publicly, uncondemned men
who are Roman citizens, and have thrown us into
prison; and do they now cast us out secretly? No! let
them come themselves and take us out." Hearing
this, the magistrates came and apologized to them
and asked them to leave the city. They left the prison,
and went to the house of Lydia who had heard their
preaching at the riverside. Impressed by what she
heard, for she was a believer and worshipper of God,
she had been baptized along with her household. In
her house the group of believers quickly came
together, were encouraged by Paul and Silas, and set
them on their way to Salonika (Acts 16:11–17:1). The
memory of that remarkable day must have often
been in Paul's mind as he faced the adventures ahead.
It is no wonder that he had a special affection for the
Philippian Christians and they for him.

Luke at the end of his second book says that Paul
was a prisoner for two years, but was allowed to live
in his own hired house, welcoming all who came to
him, preaching the Kingdom of God and teaching
about the Lord Jesus Christ, quite openly and unhin-
dered. Some of us would wonder where he got the
money for this almost private establishment. He was
proudly independent, and insisted in his free years on
earning his own keep by weaving tent cloth. We do
not know if he was permitted to do this in prison.
We do know that he would only allow the Christians
of Philippi to send him money and he was grateful
when a messenger brought gifts. It is possible Luke
his doctor friend could have practised and earned

enough for both of them by treating sick people. In some way or other he managed to keep going for two years, when it seemed likely that he was released – for a time!

It would seem clear that Paul suffered more imprisonments than those that are specifically mentioned and geographically located in the New Testament. In his list of sufferings undergone on behalf of Christ in the second letter to the Corinthians he concludes, "far more imprisonments" than those who opposed his claim to apostleship (11:23). He is implying more than he previously spoke of where he commends himself as a servant of God (6.5).

We do not know a great deal about Paul after the two years mentioned in the closing verses of the book of Acts. So we have to deduce his personal history from the letters thought to have been written from that first imprisonment or a later one. These comprise Ephesians, Philippians, Colossians and Philemon.

In the first chapter of Philippians he speaks of having a warm place in his heart for those to whom he is writing, because they have shared the grace of God in his imprisonment. He tells them how this has advanced the gospel:

> I want you to know, brethren, that what has happened to me has really served to advance the gospel, so that it has become known throughout the whole praetorian guard and to all the rest that my imprisonment is for Christ;

and most of the brethren have been made confident in the Lord because of my imprisonment, and are much more bold to speak the word of God without fear. (1:12–14)

He hopes that whether by life or death Christ will be honoured in whatever happens to his body, adding:

Yet which I shall choose I cannot tell. I am hard pressed between the two. My desire is to depart and be with Christ, for that is far better. But to remain in the flesh is more necessary on your account. Convinced of this, I know that I shall remain and continue with you all, for your progress and joy in the faith, so that in me you may have ample cause to glory in Christ Jesus, because of my coming to you again. (1:22b–26)

He sends back Epaphroditus the messenger whom they had sent with gifts for his support and who had become very ill in Rome. He does not want them to be anxious about him or about himself. The touching and affectionate passage, involving the friends at Philippi, faithful Epaphroditus and Paul himself, shows the mutual concern and loving relationship. It can be read in full in chapter 2:25–30.

He ends this happy epistle with a greeting to every disciple, from himself to those in the Emperor's household who have become Christians, and ends with a lovely little prayer that has been used all down the centuries when Christians gather together for worship.

> Greet every saint in Christ Jesus. The brethren
> who are with me greet you. All the saints
> greet you, especially those of Caesar's house-
> hold. The grace of the Lord Jesus Christ be
> with your spirit. (4:21–23)

In the letter to the churches around Ephesus, the
hypothesis of its circular nature is supported by the
fact that some of the early documents omit the
words, "in Ephesus". Definite mention of Paul as a
prisoner at the time of writing is seen in 3:1 where
he says that he is "a prisoner for Christ Jesus on
behalf of you Gentiles", and again in 4:1 where he
urges his readers to live a life worthy of their high
calling, marked by humility, love and eagerness to
preserve unity in a "relationship of peace given by
the Spirit".

In 6:14–20 it seems likely that he was thinking of
the accoutrements of the soldier detailed to guard
him, adapting each to the spiritual life and struggle
of believers. He urges his readers to be strong in the
strength of God, putting on the whole armour supplied by Him, aware that our warfare is a spiritual
one against spiritual attacks. There is to be a belt of
truth, a breastplate of righteousness and shoes ena-
bling the wearer to be quick in the cause of peace.
There is also a shield of faith, trust with which to
ward off fiery darts from evil powers, and a helmet
of salvation to protect the head and brain. These are
all protective weapons. The only attacking one is the
sword of the Spirit, which is the divine word and
direction spoken within the heart.

Finally he urges prayer in every situation, and intercession for himself that he may speak with courage in explaining the secret of the good news, "for which I am an ambassador in chains". He closes with the assurance that "the beloved brother" Tychicus will tell them everything about his circumstances, which will encourage their hearts. The last two verses of the letter are his own prayer for them:

> Peace be to the brethren, and love with faith,
> from God the Father and the Lord Jesus
> Christ. Grace be with all who love our Lord
> Jesus Christ with love undying. (6:23–24)

Colosse was a church that Paul himself had not founded. The letter to the Christians there was entrusted to Tychicus also in words similar to the ending of Ephesians, as a reading of 4:7–9 will make clear. A messenger, Epaphras, had arrived from Colosse with disturbing news, so Paul writes of his own understanding and experience of Christ. "He is the image of the invisible God, the first-born of all creation" (1:15). "In Christ, the Godhead in all its fulness is embodied, and we are filled with God through our union with Christ. He is the supreme power over all powers" (2:9–10).

When we are in Christ, we are dead as regards our old life, and can then be risen to new life with Him:

> If you have been raised with Christ, seek the
> things that are above where Christ is, seated
> at the right hand of God. Set your minds on

things that are above, not on things that are
on earth. For you have died, and your life is
hid with Christ in God. When Christ who is
our life appears, then you will also appear with
him in glory. (3:1–4)

Paul then goes on to describe the new life, as it affects
wives and husbands, masters and slaves, parents and
children. Our discipleship rises above all human
divisions (3:11), controlled by one great principle:

And whatever you do in word or deed, do
everything in the name of the Lord Jesus,
giving thanks to God the Father through him.
(3:17)

Paul dictated his letters to an amanuensis, but concludes this one with just three short sentences written
in his own hand:

I Paul, write this greeting with my own hand.
Remember my fetters. Grace be with you.
(4:18)

The shortest of the four letters written from prison
is a personal and affectionate one written to a slave
owner, Philemon, in Colosse. In it he appeals for a
runaway slave, Onesimus, "my child, whose father I
have become in my imprisonment . . . I am sending
him back to you, sending my very heart". The
punishment for a runaway slave if caught was often
death, so it was a daring thing on Paul's part to send
Onesimus back, and a brave thing for Onesimus to

consent to go. In the endearing relationship which had sprung up between the prisoner and the slave, both had come to know one another deeply. Paul also knew Philemon well, and trusted him. The triple relationship of love and trust had every hope of success.

In his letter Paul goes on to say that he would have been glad to keep the runaway with him, for he had become so useful. He even suggested that the result of it all could be that there would be a completely new relationship, very different to that of owner and slave, more like beloved brothers, the relationship which already existed between himself and Philemon. He looks upon him as a partner in an enterprise between two disciples, inspired by their mutual Lord. Paul also recognized that in the past Onesimus had been dishonest, so he promises to make good any such loss. He then reminds Philemon that he owes a great deal to himself, his very own self, the new self that he has become in Christ. He is confident that Philemon will do even more than he asks. He appeals to him, "refresh my heart in Christ".

Finally he expresses his own hope to be released and his intention to visit Colosse if and when that happens. We may note that Paul was not without friends at the time of writing, for he sends greetings from a fellow prisoner, and from Mark, Luke and two others. Philemon's home was evidently a gathering place for Christians. In Paul's opening greetings he mentions "Apphia our sister", probably Philemon's wife. He puts his usual prayerful blessing at the beginning of his letter: "Grace to you and peace from God our Father and the Lord Jesus Christ."

I can well imagine that the Bible and Gospel loving William Wilberforce, nearly eighteen centuries later, found inspiration from this letter, as he committed himself to work for the abolition of the slave trade and the emancipation of slaves everywhere.

We are given a last self-revelatory insight into a second imprisonment in Rome in what purports to be the second epistle to Timothy, whom Paul addressed as "my beloved child". Scholars differ as to their views of whether Paul was the actual writer of this pastoral epistle, or whether it was the work of an interpreter of Paul. One cannot doubt that it seems true to what we know of him from the book of Acts and from the undisputed epistles. Let it stand without comment:

> For I am already on the point of being sacrificed; the time of my departure has come. I have fought the good fight, I have finished the race, I have kept the faith. Henceforth there is laid up for me the crown of righteousness, which the Lord, the righteous judge, will award to me on that Day, and not only to me but also to all who have loved his appearing. (2 Timothy 4:6–8)

14

The Prayers of Paul

It would be a bad mistake to think that Paul did not value and practise prayer before he became a disciple of Jesus and acknowledged him to be the long-expected Messiah. He was born in a deeply religious family, strong in the beliefs and ways of worship of the Pharisees, and sent to be trained as a rabbi under Gamaliel, an outstanding teacher. He would have been a strict observer of the sabbath and the services connected with it, keeping the festivals and fasts of the calendar and the prescribed visits to Jerusalem, as well as ceremonies connected with the home such as circumcision and passover. Well before his visit to Damascus he would have undertaken rabbinical duties. He would have been not only aware of the prayers in synagogue, home and temple, but often called upon to lead them. In his mission journeys he made a practice of going first to the synagogues, joining in the worship, and meeting the Jewish community in each place.

His very first prayer after the shattering experience on the outskirts of Damascus was a very short act of surrender which was to be the chief principle of his life:

Lord, what wilt Thou have me to do? (Acts 22:10 AV)

It was also a proof to him of what as a Pharisee he had always professed, namely resurrection, in this case of one who had been executed as a heretic and criminal. The first word of it is the most significant, the rest of it expresses its implication, meaning and intention.

The study of his letters, roughly in the order in which they were written, is very revealing of his inner spiritual life. The two Epistles to the Christians of Salonika are thought to be his earliest. They contain three prayers which are as relevant to us today as they were to Paul himself and to those who would read his disclosure of their content and wording:

> Now may our God and Father himself, and our Lord Jesus, direct our way to you; and may the Lord make you increase and abound in love to one another and to all men, as we do to you, so that he may establish your hearts unblameable in holiness before our God and Father, at the coming of our Lord Jesus with all his saints. (1 Thessalonians 3:11–13)

> May the God of peace himself sanctify you wholly; and may your spirit and soul and body be kept sound and blameless at the coming of our Lord Jesus Christ. (1 Thessalonians 5:23)

Now may our Lord Jesus Christ himself, and God our Father, who loved us and gave us eternal comfort and good hope through grace, comfort your hearts and establish them in every good work and word. (2 Thessalonians 2:16–17)

In his first letter to the Christians of Corinth, written about AD 57, Paul gives thanks to God for the grace which has enriched their lives:

I give thanks to God always for you because of the grace of God which was given you in Christ Jesus, that in every way you were enriched in him with all speech and all knowledge – even as the testimony to Christ was confirmed among you – so that you are not lacking in any spiritual gift, as you wait for the revealing of our Lord Jesus Christ. God is faithful, by whom you were called into the fellowship of his Son, Jesus Christ our Lord. (1 Corinthians 1:4–9)

In his second letter written shortly afterwards he blesses God for his strengthening grace in all difficulties and sufferings:

Blessed be the God and Father of our Lord Jesus Christ, the Father of mercies and God of all comfort, who comforts us in all our affliction, so that we may be able to comfort those who are in any affliction, with the comfort with which we ourselves are comforted by

God. For as we share abundantly in Christ's sufferings, so through Christ we share abundantly in comfort too. (2 Corinthians 1:3–5)

Paul ends this inspiring letter with one of the best known prayers which is used even today at the end of intercessions in most services or at the conclusion of worship. Just one sentence, known from its opening words as "The Grace":

The grace of the Lord Jesus Christ and the love of God and the fellowship of the Holy Spirit be with you all. (2 Corinthians 13:14)

Even in his reproachful letter written from Corinth in 57–58 AD to the Galatians who have been straying from the original gospel which they had received from him, Paul opens with a thankful note:

Grace to you and peace from God the Father and our Lord Jesus Christ, who gave himself for our sins to deliver us from the present evil age, according to the will of our God and Father; to whom be the glory for ever and ever. Amen. (Galatians 1:3–5)

In his epistle to the Christians in Rome, written at much the same time as Galatians, Paul tells of his prayer that he will at long last succeed in visiting the capital of the empire:

First, I thank my God through Jesus Christ for all of you, because your faith is proclaimed in all the world. For God is my witness, whom I

serve with my spirit in the gospel of his Son,
that without ceasing I mention you always in
my prayers, asking that somehow by God's
will I may now at last succeed in coming to
you. For I long to see you, that I may impart
to you some spiritual gift to strengthen you,
that is, that we may be mutually encouraged
by each other's faith, both yours and mine.
(Romans 1:8–12)

In the same Epistle, Paul has a lovely Gloria to God,
the source of all wisdom and knowledge:

O the depths of the riches and wisdom and
knowledge of God! How unsearchable are his
judgments and how inscrutable his ways! For
who has known the mind of the Lord, or who
has been his counsellor? Or who has given a
gift to him that he might be repaid? For from
him and through him and to him are all things.
To him be glory for ever. Amen. (Romans
11:33–36)

During the two years 61–63, in which he was
under military guard in Rome, Paul took advantage
of his enforced leisure to write four epistles – Colossians, Ephesians, Philippians and Philemon. He prays
for the Colossian Christians:

We have not ceased to pray that you may be
filled with the knowledge of his will in all
spiritual wisdom and understanding, to lead a
life worthy of the Lord, fully pleasing to him,

bearing fruit in every good work and increasing in the knowledge of God. May you be strengthened with all power, according to his glorious might, for all endurance and patience with joy, giving thanks to the Father, who has qualified us to share in the inheritance of the saints in light. (1:9–12)

He ends the Colossian letter in his own handwriting with a short request and a short prayer:

Remember my fetters. Grace be with you. (4:18)

He opens his letter to the Ephesians with a prayerful greeting and a blessing of God for his eternal choice, grace and calling:

Blessed be the God and Father of our Lord Jesus Christ, who has blessed us in Christ with every spiritual blessing in the heavenly places, even as he chose us in him before the foundation of the world, that we should be holy and blameless before him. He destined us in love to be his sons through Jesus Christ, according to the purpose of his will, to the praise of his glorious grace which he freely bestowed on us in the Beloved. (1:3–6)

Later he prays a prayer for them, whose four-dimensional relevance, spiritual depth and fulness cannot be measured:

I bow my knees before the Father, from whom every family in heaven and on earth is named, that according to the riches of his glory he may grant you to be strengthened with might through his Spirit in the inner man, and that Christ may dwell in your hearts through faith; that you, being rooted and grounded in love, may have power to comprehend with all the saints what is the breadth and length and height and depth, and to know the love of Christ which surpasses knowledge, that you may be filled with all the fulness of God. Now to him who by the power at work within us is able to do far more abundantly than all that we ask or think to him be glory in the church and in Christ Jesus to all generations, for ever and ever. Amen. (3:14–21)

For the Philippians he thanks God with joyful remembrance of them and prays that their love may abound more and more, with holy living:

I thank my God in all my remembrance of you, always in every prayer of mine for you all making my prayer with joy, thankful for your partnership in the gospel from the first day until now. And I am sure that he who began a good work in you will bring it to completion at the day of Jesus Christ. It is right for me to feel thus about you all, because I hold you in my heart, for you are all partakers with me of grace, both in my imprisonment and in the defence and confirmation of

the gospel. For God is my witness, how I
yearn for you all with the affection of Christ
Jesus. And it is my prayer that your love may
abound more and more, with knowledge and
all discernment, so that you may approve what
is excellent and may be pure and blameless for
the day of Christ, filled with all the fruits of
righteousness which come through Jesus
Christ, to the glory and praise of God.
(1:3–11)

The personal and pastoral letter to Timothy has a
lovely Gloria in which we today often express our
faith and worship.

The King of kings and Lord of lords, who
alone has immortality and dwells in unapproachable light, whom no man has ever seen
or can see. To him be honour and eternal
dominion. Amen. (1 Timothy 6:15b–16)

In the epistle to Titus, "my true child in a common
faith", Paul prays:

Grace and peace from God the Father and
Jesus Christ our Saviour. (1:4)

He ends:

All who are with me send their greetings to
you. Greet those who love us in the faith.
Grace be with you all. (3:15)

Paul often asks those to whom he is writing to
pray for him:

Pray at all times in the Spirit, with all prayer and supplication. To that end keep alert with all perseverance, making supplication for all the saints, and also for me, that utterance may be given me in opening my mouth boldly to proclaim the mystery of the gospel, for which I am an ambassador in chains; that I may declare it boldly, as I ought to speak. (Ephesians 6:18–20)

I appeal to you brethren, by our Lord Jesus Christ and by the love of the Spirit, to strive together with me in your prayers to God on my behalf, that I may be delivered from the unbelievers in Judea, and that my service for Jerusalem may be acceptable to the saints, so that by God's will I may come to you with joy and be refreshed in your company. The God of peace be with you all. Amen. (Romans 15:30–33)

You also must help us by prayer, so that many will give thanks on our behalf for the blessing granted us in answer to many prayers. (2 Corinthians 1:11)

Prayer to Paul was more than voiced prayers for those brought to God through his preaching and personal influence, or in his letters informing them of the content of what he prayed. It was also being aware of the divine presence at all times and in all places, opening heart and mind to the divine guidance, listening to any communication from God which would reveal the divine will and give grace to carry it out, revealing the right response to God-given insights and opportunities, even in dangers and emergencies.

This may be seen in situations recorded by Luke in the book of Acts, who must have heard from Paul of his own deep spiritual experiences in them. Thus, in Acts 16:6–8 when the next step forward was not clear and all possible ways seemed blocked, he writes:

> And they went through the region of Phrygia and Galatia, having been forbidden by the Holy Spirit to speak the word in Asia. And when they had come opposite Mysia, they attempted to go into Bithynia, but the Spirit of Jesus did not allow them; so, passing by Mysia, they went down to Troas.

And again, in the face of hostile opposition in Corinth:

> And the Lord said to Paul one night in a vision, "Do not be afraid, but speak and do not be silent; for I am with you, and no man shall attack you to harm you; for I have many people in this city." (18:9–10)

And in the violent storm on the journey to Rome:

> And as they had been long without food, Paul then came forward among them and said, "Men, you should have listened to me, and should not have set sail from Crete and

incurred this injury and loss. I now bid you take heart; for there will be no loss of life among you, but only of the ship. For this very night there stood by me an angel of the God to whom I belong and whom I worship, and he said, 'Do not be afraid, Paul; you must stand before Caesar; and lo, God has granted you all those who sail with you.' So take heart, men, for I have faith in God that it will be exactly as I have been told." (27:21–25)

Paul also speaks of deep spiritual experience in his prayer and meditation:

I will go on to visions and revelations of the Lord. I know a man in Christ who fourteen years ago was caught up to the third heaven – whether in the body or out of the body I do not know, God knows. And I know that this man was caught up into Paradise – whether in the body or out of the body I do not know, God knows – and he heard things that cannot be told, which man may not utter. (2 Corinthians 12:1b–4)

He speaks of an early experience while praying in the Temple on his return to Jerusalem from Damascus:

When I had returned to Jerusalem and was praying in the temple, I fell into a trance and saw him saying to me, "Make haste and get quickly out of Jerusalem, because they will not accept your testimony about me." And I said, "Lord, they themselves know that in every synagogue I imprisoned and beat those who believed in thee. And when the blood of Stephen thy witness was shed, I also was standing by and approving, and keeping the garments of those who killed him." And he said to me, "Depart; for I will send you far away to the Gentiles." (Acts 22:17–21)

Paul does not deal at length with difficulties in prayer, but in his epistle to the Romans, he hints at our inability to pray as we ought:

Likewise the Spirit helps us in our weakness; for we do not know how to pray as we ought, but the Spirit himself intercedes for us with sighs too deep for words. And he who searches the hearts of men knows what is the mind of the Spirit, because the Spirit intercedes for the saints according to the Will of God. (8:26–27)

If we have the Spirit in us, He intercedes for us when thoughts and words fail. The phrase, "with sighs too deep for words" can be a comfort when we are struck with our own weakness or with the tragedies and crimes of the world. At such moments a sigh may be all that we can manage, and may make clear to God both our dismay and our inability to express our inner feelings in an acceptable way.

Paul gives us one instance when he felt that God had not answered an earnest and often repeated prayer:

> And to keep me from being too elated by the abundance of revelations, a thorn was given me in the flesh, a messenger of Satan, to harass me, to keep me from being too elated. Three times I besought the Lord about this, that it should leave me; but he said to me, "My grace is sufficient for you, for my power is made perfect in weakness." I will all the more gladly boast of my weaknesses, that the power of Christ may rest upon me. (2 Corinthians 12:7–9)

I, and perhaps many others, may have wondered if Paul's interpretation of the "thorn in the flesh" was a right one, thinking that whatever it was came from God or the devil, even if it was meant to prevent him getting over-elated with the many revelations he had received. But what he heard from God rings true in what we know about God from the gospels or in our own prayer life. God's grace is always sufficient if we are ready and eager to receive it. God's power gets its greatest opportunity when we recognize our weakness and need.

Such experience will keep us from getting too proud or boastful of our own achievements, and inspire us to be confident and trustful in Him – and deeply thankful for his grace and power, and for all He says to us at the deepest level of our spirits.

Texts from Paul to meditate upon:

Lord, what wilt Thou have me to do? (Acts 22:10 AV)

I can do all things in Christ who strengthens me. (Philippians 4:13)

My strength is made perfect in weakness. (2 Corinthians 12:9)

Nothing will be able to separate us from the love of God in Christ Jesus, our Lord. (Romans 8:39)

If anyone is in Christ, he is a new creature (a new creation). (2 Corinthians 5:17)

God was in Christ reconciling the world to Himself. (2 Corinthians 5:19)

God was in Christ entrusting to us the message of reconciliation. (2 Corinthians 5:19)

We are ambassadors for Christ. (2 Corinthians 5:20)

Though he was rich, for your sake he became poor, so that by his poverty you might become rich. (2 Corinthians 8:9)

Love bears all things, believes all things, endures all things. Love never ends. (1 Corinthians 13:7–8)

I count everything as loss because of the surpassing worth of knowing Christ Jesus, my Lord. (Philippians 3:8)

Have no anxiety in anything, but in everything by prayer and supplication with thanksgiving, let your requests be made known to God. (Philippians 4:6)

Our commonwealth is in heaven. (Philippians 3:20)

I have learned in whatever state I am to be content. (Philippians 4:11)

May the God of peace Himself sanctify you wholly, and may your spirit and soul and body be kept sound and blameless at the coming of our Lord Jesus. (1 Thessalonians 5:23)

God our Saviour desires all to be saved and come to the knowledge of the truth. (1 Timothy 2:4)

The love of money is the root of all evils. (1 Timothy 6:10)

Go did not give us a spirit of timidity, but a spirit of power and love and self-control. (2 Timothy 1:6–7)

We have the mind of Christ. (1 Corinthians 2:16)

Whatever is true, whatever is honourable, whatever is just, whatever is pure, whatever is lovely, whatever is gracious, if there is anything worthy of praise, think about these things. (Philippians 4:8)

Put to death what is earthly in you: immorality, impurity, passion, evil desire, and covetousness, which is idolatry. (Colossians 3:5)

Remember the words of the Lord Jesus, how he said "It is more blessed to give than to receive". (Acts 20:35)

15

An Eternal Weight of Glory

In his first letter to the Christians of Corinth Paul speaks of a glorification which God had in mind for the human race before time began and which has been made clear in Christ Jesus:

> We impart a secret and hidden wisdom of God, which God decreed before the ages of our glorification. (2:7)

He asserts that none of the rulers of the world had perceived this, and he gives his opinion that if they had done so, they could not have possibly crucified the "Lord of Glory". He quotes from the book of Isaiah:

> What no eye has seen nor ear heard, nor the heart of man conceived,
> what God has prepared for those who love Him.

Some of us would like to add, "and for those who do not yet do so", believing that to be part of the New Testament gospel. Paul tells us that the aim of every Christian disciple must be, "Whatever you do, do all to the glory of God" (1 Corinthians 10:31), not seeking our own advantage, but that of the many, that they may be saved. When we do that with careful thought and decision, leading to action and practice which will enhance God's reputation and deepen our reverence for Him and his holy will, we are hallowing God's name, as our response to the first petition of the Lord's Prayer.

At the end of a section in the epistle to the Romans in which he has been speaking of the relationship of Christian believers and continuing Jews, Paul offers a Gloria of his own:

> O the depths of the riches and wisdom and knowledge of God! How unsearchable are his judgments and how inscrutable his ways! For who has known the mind of the Lord, or who has been his counsellor? Or who has given a gift to Him that he might be repaid? For from Him and through Him and to Him are all things. To him be glory for ever. Amen. (11:33–36)

It is interesting to note that Luke, Paul's Gentile friend, tells us that it was while Jesus was praying that his face shone and there was an aura of light around his figure (9:28–36). When a cloud over-shadows the whole bright scene, a voice said to the three watching disciples, "This is my Son, my Chosen: Listen to him", echoing the voice that came to Jesus at his baptism.

In his second letter to the Corinthians Paul speaks of the transfiguration of Moses as he came down from Sinai with his face radiant because he had been talking with God (Exodus 34:33). He says that Moses put a veil over his face so that the Israelites might not see the fading splendour. He goes on: "To this day whenever Moses is read a veil lies over their minds. It is only when a man turns to the Lord the veil is removed." He concludes with the assurance of our progressive transfiguration: "We all with unveiled faces, beholding the glory of the Lord, are being changed into his likeness from one degree of glory to another" (2 Corinthians 3:18).

Returning to that second letter to the Christians of Corinth we find Paul saying:

> So we do not lose heart. Though our outer nature is wasting away, our inner nature is being renewed every day. For this slight momentary affliction is preparing for us an eternal weight of glory beyond all comparison, because we look not to the things that are seen but to the things that are unseen: for the things that are seen are transient, but the things that are unseen are eternal. (4:16–18)

> For it is the God who said, "Let light shine out of darkness", who has shone in our hearts to give the light of the knowledge of the glory of God in the face of Christ. (4:6)

Towards the end of the first letter to Timothy there is a worshipful ascription of Glory to God:

> . . . the blessed and only Sovereign, the King of kings and Lord of lords, who alone has

immortality and dwells in unapproachable
light, whom no man has ever seen or can see.
To Him be honour and eternal dominion.
Amen. (1 Timothy 6:15–16)

Paul's phrase, "an eternal weight of glory beyond all
comparison" speaks of lasting substance and significance, reminding Christians of that exquisite little
parable of the pearl of great price which is worth
giving everything to gain (Matthew 13:45–46).

Paul in his pre-conversion days, as a rabbi trained
under the famous Gamaliel, would have gained an
intimate knowledge of the Psalms, most of them
being songs of praise and worship sung in the temple
to the glory of God. Among psalms which find
echoes, if not direct quotation, in his thinking,
teaching and personal devotion, the meditating student will pick out Psalm 8, which speaks of the
relation between the Creator and the creature, the
place of man in the universe, compared with the
greatness of God and the vastness of creation.

The first three verses speak of the majesty of God,
acknowledged by angels in the spiritual sphere far
outreaching the material universe, silencing critics
and all who oppose Him – That majesty in "the
mouths of babes and sucklings", in the marvel of
human speech and the ability to express thought and
convey meaning. Man is but a babe in the universe,
a latecomer in developing creation, when compared
with the age of the earth and the eternity of God. In
the next two verses, the psalmist is conscious of

man's insignificance, as he gazes at the light coming from moon and stars. He exclaims, "What is man?" and then wonders why God should care for him or want to visit him. Verses six to nine speak of man's spiritual nature. God has made him only a little less than divine, endowing him with glory and honour, and delegating to him responsibility for the earth and its creatures. In the light of such thoughts the psalmist repeats his opening words, "O Lord our Governor", and pays a tribute of worship to God for his glorious revelation of Himself.

Another psalm speaks of the revelation of God in nature and of his disclosure in the Torah, the divine Law with its insights, its directions for moral and holy living, its commandments as to what is to be avoided and what is to be practised:

> More to be desired than much fine gold;
> sweeter also than honey dripping from the honeycomb.

The psalm ends with the prayer:

> Let the words of my mouth
> and the meditation of my heart
> be acceptable in thy sight,
> O Lord, my rock and my redeemer. (Psalm 19:10, 14)

From my not very extensive reading of the philosopher Kant I remember a quotation which sums up the message of this psalm: "There are two things that fill my soul with holy reverence and ever-growing wonder – the spectacle of the starry sky that virtually annihilates us physical beings, and the moral law which raises us to infinite dignity as intelligent agents".

A short mention of other verses in the Psalms must include Psalm 24:3–5:

> Who shall ascend the hill of the Lord? and who
>   shall stand in his holy place?
> He who has clean hands and a pure heart,
> who does not lift up his soul to what is false,
> and does not swear deceitfully.
> He will receive blessing from the Lord, and
>   vindication
> from the God of his salvation.

Psalm 104:31 has a note of eternity:

> May the glory of the Lord endure for ever,
> may the Lord rejoice in his works.

Psalm 150 is a symphony of praise:

> Praise the Lord! Praise God in his sanctuary;
> praise Him in his mighty firmament!
> Praise Him for his mighty deeds,
> praise Him according to his exceeding greatness!
> Let everything that breathes praise the Lord.
>   (Psalm 150: 1–2, 6)

Shekhinah

This glory of God is spoken of in the Hebrew Bible as Shekhinah, God's glorious dwelling in heaven and eternity, his loving presence in the world with all who seek Him and even his unobserved presence with those who do not yet seek Him. An early reference to it may be seen in Exodus 25:8, where Moses legislating for the worship of the newly liberated people from slavery in Egypt hears the divine voice saying to him: "Let them make me a sanctuary, that I may dwell in their midst". In Leviticus 16:16 speaking of the sprinkling of the blood of the goat of the sin offering as part of the ritual for the Day of Atonement: "Aaron shall make atonement for the holy place, because of the uncleanness of the people of Israel and because of their transgression, all their sins". According to the teaching of successive generations of the rabbis, conversion to Judaism is called, "being brought under the wings of the Shekhinah".

In his experience at the Burning Bush, Moses recognizes that he is in the divine presence, standing on holy ground. So he takes off his shoes as a gesture of reverence and worship. He then hears God telling him to return to Egypt to liberate his people, and he asks what name will give authority and authenticity to his mission and message. He is told to reply, "I

AM has sent me to you", adding, "I AM WHAT I AM", implying that no one can define the divine mystery of God's Being and Activity. The Hebrew words have been interpreted in early manuscripts of the books of Exodus as, "I WILL BE WHAT I WILL BE", indicating God's indescribable and unpredictable nature. Martin Buber, the great Jewish scholar and philosopher (1878–1965), who seems to have been more appreciated by Christians, translates the Hebrew, 'I WILL BE THERE", indicating a presence in Egypt as well as at Sinai, and a presence that will accompany Moses on his journey and in his activity among the enslaved people of God in Egypt.

The Shekhinah may rest upon individuals or be glimpsed by them. Jacob fleeing from his brother whom he had cheated of his birthright, on his first night away from home, had his wonderful dream of a stairway to heaven, with the angels of God ascending and descending on it, with God standing above it assuring him of his presence. When he awoke he said, "Surely the Lord is in this place and I did not know it . . . How awesome is this place! This is none other than the house of God, and this is the gate of heaven" (Genesis 28:12–17).

Isaiah at a morning sacrifice in the Temple, "saw the Lord, sitting upon a throne, high and lifted up: and his train filled the Temple". He heard the song of the seraphim, the angels of his presence, "Holy, holy, holy is the Lord of hosts; the whole earth is full of his glory!" His first reaction was one of dismay: "Woe is me! For I am lost; for I am a man of unclean lips". Then in his vision he saw one of the seraphs fly towards him with a burning coal in his hand taken from the altar, and putting it to his lips with the words, "Your guilt is taken away, and your sin forgiven". A moment later Isaiah hears the divine voice ask, "Whom shall I send, and who will go for us?" Fortified by the vision of glory and the assurance of forgiveness and cleansing, the young man responds, "Here am I! Send me" (Isaiah 6:1–8).

Ezekiel in exile in Babylon has a vision in which four living creatures symbolizing strength, speed like a hurricane moving straight forward, full of eyes signifying knowledge, facing the four points of the compass suggesting that all parts of the universe are open to the gaze of God. The vision is not easy for the reader to understand, for the prophet is trying to describe the Indescribable. In another vision he sees the divine glory hovering over Jerusalem and moving to Babylon, an assurance that the Shekhinah is with his people in exile. Yet another vision promises return and restoration of the city, temple and daily worship. A further spiritual experience describes a river of life rising in the Temple and flowing through the desert, getting deeper and stronger, with trees on both banks, and finally entering the Dead Sea, so that its waters are healed and swarm with all kinds of fish. The trees on the shore bear fruit every month and their leaves have healing porperties. This vision of the river of life is taken up by the writer of the book of Revelation. Michael Ramsey used to emphasize that we need to be quiet and passive, and open to receive the great stream of God's love and compassion.

The *Encyclopedia of Jewish Religion* describes the kind of spirit which prepares for the coming of the divine glory into human lives: "The Shekhinah rests upon man not through gloom, indolence, frivolity or idle chatter, but only through the joy experienced in fulfilling Divine Commandments. The Shekhinah is present in every home where there is domestic peace, and blesses that home. Study and congregational prayer bring about the presence of the Shekhinah, whereas sin and injustice drive it away. When Israel goes into exile the Shekhinah accompanies them and it will accompany them on their return. The bliss of the beatific vision in the future world is expressed in the words, 'there the righteous sit and enjoy the splendor of the Shekhinah.'"

Luke, meditating on the birth of Jesus, speaking of the shepherds in the fields around Bethlehem on that most blessed night, says: "the glory of the Lord shone round about them" (2:9). Luke also describes a night on Mount Tabor (or possibly Hermon) which Jesus spent with his three most intimate disciples:

> As he was praying, the appearance of his countenance was altered, and his raiment became dazzling white and behold two men walked with him, Moses and Elijah, who appeared in glory and spoke of his departure, which he was to accomplish in Jerusalem.

Peter and his two companions were able on that occasion to keep awake:

> . . . and they saw his glory and the two men
> who stood with him. (Luke 9:28–35)

The divine glory was shining through Jesus in a
transfiguration which convinced the three watching
disciples that he was indeed the beloved Son of God.

The apostle John in exile on the island of Patmos
had an experience of the divine glory:

> I was in the Spirit on the Lord's Day, and I
> heard behind me a loud voice like a trumpet
> . . . Then I turned to see the voice that was
> speaking to me, and on turning I saw seven
> golden lampstands, and in the midst of the
> lampstands one like a son of man, clothed
> with a long robe and with a golden girdle
> round his breast; his head and his hair were
> white as white wool, white as snow; his eyes
> were like a flame of fire, his feet were like
> burnished bronze, refined as in a furnace, and
> his voice was like the sound of many waters;
> in his right hand he held seven stars, from his
> mouth issued a sharp two-edged sword, and
> his face was like the sun shining in full
> strength. (Revelation 1:12–16)

The Shekhinah not only shone through Jesus, but
rested on John also, convincing him that Jesus was
alive for evermore and that he held the keys to both
life and death. John continues:

> After this I looked, and lo, in heaven an open
> door! And the first voice, which I had heard

speaking to me like a trumpet, said, "Come up hither, and I will show you what must take place after this." At once I was in the Spirit, and lo, a throne stood in heaven, with one seated on the throne! And he who sat there appeared like jasper and carnelian, and round the throne was a rainbow that looked like an emerald. Round the throne were twenty-four thrones, and seated on the thrones were twenty-four elders, clad in white garments, with golden crowns upon their heads. (Revelation 4:1–4)

Matthew in his collection of our Lord's teaching in what is called the Sermon on the Mount, tells his disciples:

You are the light of the world. A city set on a hill cannot be hid. Nor do men light a lamp and put it under a bushel, but on a stand, and it gives light to all in the house. Let your light so shine before men, that they may see your good works and give glory to your Father who is in heaven. (Matthew 5:14–16)

Pamela Vermes concludes her great book on Martin Buber with a lovely quotation from a poem of D. H. Lawrence:

Sleeping on the hearth of the living world
yawning at home before the fire of life
feeling the presence of the living God
like a great reassurance

of deep calm in the heart
a presence
as of the master sitting at the board
of his own greater being
in the house of life.

An ancient Latin collect, translated in the Anglican *Book of Common Prayer*, can appropriately conclude this whole book of meditations on the Apostle Paul:

O God, who hast prepared for them that love thee such good things as pass man's understanding: Pour into our hearts such love toward thee, that we, loving thee above all things, may obtain thy promises, which exceed all that we can desire: through Jesus Christ our Lord. Amen.

Also available in Fount Paperbacks

The Mind of St Paul
WILLIAM BARCLAY

'There is a deceptive simplicity about this fine exposition of Pauline thought at once popular and deeply theological. The Hebrew and Greek backgrounds are described and all the main themes are lightly but fully treated.' *The Yorkshire Post*

The Plain Man Looks at the Beatitudes
WILLIAM BARCLAY

'. . . the author's easy style should render it . . . valuable and acceptable to the ordinary reader.' *Church Times*

The Plain Man Looks at the Lord's Prayer
WILLIAM BARCLAY

Professor Barclay shows how this prayer that Jesus gave to his disciples is at once a summary of Christian teaching and a pattern for all prayers.

The Plain Man's Guide to Ethics
WILLIAM BARCLAY

The author demonstrates beyond all possible doubt that the Ten Commandments are the most relevant document in the world today and are totally related to mankind's capacity to live and make sense of it all within a Christian context.

Ethics in a Permissive Society
WILLIAM BARCLAY

How do we as Christians deal with such problems as drug taking, the 'pill', alcohol, morality of all kinds, in a society whose members are often ignorant of the Church's teaching? Professor Barclay approaches a difficult and vexed question with his usual humanity and clarity, asking what Christ himself would say or do in our world today.

Also available in Fount Paperbacks

I Believe
Trevor Huddleston

A simple, prayerful series of reflections on the phrases of the Creed. This is a beautiful testament of the strong, quiet inner faith of a man best known for his active role in the Church – and in the world.

The Heart of the Christian Faith
Donald Coggan

The author ". . . presents the essential core of Christianity in a marvellously simple and readable form, quite uncluttered by any excess of theological technicality."

The Yorkshire Post

Be Still and Know
Michael Ramsey

The former Archbishop of Canterbury looks at prayer in the New Testament, at what the early mystics could teach us about it, and at some practical aspects of Christian praying.

Pilgrim's Progress
John Bunyan

"A masterpiece which generation after generation of ordinary men and women have taken to their hearts."

Hugh Ross Williamson

Fount Paperbacks

Fount is one of the leading paperback publishers of religious books and below are some of its recent titles.

- ☐ FRIENDSHIP WITH GOD David Hope £2.95
- ☐ THE DARK FACE OF REALITY Martin Israel £2.95
- ☐ LIVING WITH CONTRADICTION Esther de Waal £2.95
- ☐ FROM EAST TO WEST Brigid Marlin £3.95
- ☐ GUIDE TO THE HERE AND HEREAFTER
                              Lionel Blue/Jonathan Magonet £4.50
- ☐ CHRISTIAN ENGLAND (1 Vol) David Edwards £10.95
- ☐ MASTERING SADHANA Carlos Valles £3.95
- ☐ THE GREAT GOD ROBBERY George Carey £2.95
- ☐ CALLED TO ACTION Fran Beckett £2.95
- ☐ TENSIONS Harry Williams £2.50
- ☐ CONVERSION Malcolm Muggeridge £2.95
- ☐ INVISIBLE NETWORK Frank Wright £2.95
- ☐ THE DANCE OF LOVE Stephen Verney £3.95
- ☐ THANK YOU, PADRE Joan Clifford £2.50
- ☐ LIGHT AND LIFE Grazyna Sikorska £2.95
- ☐ CELEBRATION Margaret Spufford £2.95
- ☐ GOODNIGHT LORD Georgette Butcher £2.95
- ☐ GROWING OLDER Una Kroll £2.95

All Fount Paperbacks are available at your bookshop or newsagent, or they can be ordered by post from Fount Paperbacks, Cash Sales Department, G.P.O. Box 29, Douglas, Isle of Man. Please send purchase price plus 22p per book, maximum postage £3. Customers outside the UK send purchase price, plus 22p per book. Cheque, postal order or money order. No currency.

NAME (Block letters) _____

ADDRESS_____

_____

_____